PRAISE FOR
SUCCESS AS A

"This book will serve as an indispensable 'mentor on the desk' for any ambitious coach. An excellent guide on your journey to successfully running your own business." **Sue Mitchell, chartered accountant and former in-house executive coach at KPMG, now owner of specialist coaching business**

"If you want to make a success of your coaching business, look no further than this no-nonsense, intelligent and practical guide from someone who has been there and done that with aplomb." **Anne Scoular, MD of Meyler Campbell and author of** *The FT Guide to Business Coaching*

"It's one thing getting your coaching or professional qualification, but something completely different setting yourself up in business. Stephen uses his experienced coach's knack of asking the reader powerful questions to take you through all the vital steps. He combines this engaging style with a considerable amount of practical advice from years of professional success, in an up-to-date book that is straightforward, readable and detailed. An invaluable resource for coaches – or any professionals – wanting to make the most of their expertise with paying clients." **Stefan Cantore, Senior Teaching Fellow in Organizational Behaviour & Human Resource Management at the Management School University of Southampton, executive coach/OD consultant and author of** *Top 50 Business Psychology Models*

"A must read for any new or established executive coach who is seeking a clear and no-nonsense manual for client acquisition and creating their own financially successful coaching practice." **Dr Henry Ford, executive coach to the City of London, former Director of a €10B PE Fund Investment Committee and Managing Director at Citigroup, www.CaptainMomentum.com**

"An invaluable roadmap that will help you navigate the key strategic and logistical decisions to be considered when setting up as a coach, providing proven advice on how to sustain your business and maximize profitability. This comprehensive reference allows you to benefit from years of 'in the field' experience in order to expand your professional network, finesse your marketing efforts and optimize client relationships. Whether you are new to coaching or established in the field, this book is guaranteed to save you precious time and make a felt difference to your bottom line." **Harriet Farmer, PR Director and coach-in-training**

Success
as a Coach

Success as a Coach

Start and build a successful coaching practice

Stephen Newton

KoganPage

LONDON   PHILADELPHIA   NEW DELHI

Publisher's note

Every possible effort has been made to ensure that the information contained in this book is accurate at the time of going to press, and the publisher and author cannot accept responsibility for any errors or omissions, however caused. No responsibility for loss or damage occasioned to any person acting, or refraining from action, as a result of the material in this publication can be accepted by the editor, the publisher or the author.

First published in Great Britain and the United States in 2013 by Kogan Page Limited

2nd Floor, 45 Gee Street
London EC1V 3RS
United Kingdom
www.koganpage.com

1518 Walnut Street, Suite 11000
Philadelphia PA 19102
USA

4737/23 Ansari Road
Daryaganj
New Delhi 110002
India

© Stephen Newton, 2013

ISBN   978 0 7494 6909 2
E-ISBN   978 0 7494 6910 8

British Library Cataloguing-in-Publication Data

A CIP record for this book is available from the British Library.

Library of Congress Cataloging-in-Publication Data

Newton, Stephen.
    Success as a coach : start and build a successful coaching practice / Stephen Newton.
        pages cm
    ISBN 978-0-7494-6909-2 (pbk.) – ISBN 978-0-7494-6910-8 (ebook)   1. Executive coaching.
2. Mentoring in business.   3. New business enterprises–Management.   4. Small business–
Management.   I. Title.
    HD30.4.N475 2013
    658.4'07124–dc23

                                                                                                                2013022888

Typeset by Graphicraft Limited, Hong Kong
Printed and bound in India by Replika Press Pvt Ltd

CONTENTS

Introduction

Let's take it as read that you can coach and have relevant training. For a coach, success comes in two parts:

1 delivering massive value for clients (and the resulting personal fulfilment); and

2 being able to build a healthy and growing practice with the consequent financial reward.

The second item is in fact an outcome of the first.

The factors that drive the achievement of the first are by no means all to do with your ability as a coach. In fact your coaching ability is essentially a hygiene factor; something that the client assumes. The key to success as a coach is client acquisition (supported by client retention).

You need to get in front of the right kind of clients so that you can gain agreement to work together and succeed by exercising your coaching expertise. Hence you deliver massive value for the clients who become instant and powerful references for you. Note the word choice: this is not simply a question of client acquisition, but the acquisition of the right clients for you. This applies not only to those coaches who seek to work as an independent but also to those who plan to coach in-house: same strategic issue but different tactics required.

The client is not usually interested in the coaching process as such – just the results. Therefore your coaching process should be as invisible as possible unless the client asks you to explain what is going on and why.

In this book we explore how to develop a successful business as an independent business coach. The approaches outlined here have been developed and proved in the field over more than a decade.

We look at how to identify and then connect with as many of the right kind of clients for you as you can handle (extending your professional network). That is not the same as the maximum number of possible clients; that would be a machine-gun approach as opposed to single, carefully aimed shots from a sniper's rifle.

Many people in business need a good coach whether they know it or not. The majority of them will not be right for you, however, no matter how tempting it may be to take them on as a client simply in order to bring in some revenue. The downside is that the 'wrong' clients will take time that could be better used and create stress that you don't need. If these 'poor' or 'difficult' clients refer others to you at all, 'like refers like' and those referrals will tend to be similar friction generators.

We look at how to identify what drives 'good' clients at an emotional level (which is where they take decisions), how they take buying decisions and the way they prefer to receive information. Armed with that information, you can then outline in language that resonates with that person the benefits of working with you. The result is to maximize the likelihood that the client can and will say 'yes'. It also differentiates you from other coaches and minimizes price as an issue in the client's buying decision.

We shall explore how to answer the three great killer questions. The first of these is 'What do you do?'. It must be responded to in a way that answers the client's unspoken question, which is 'Why do I need to take the time to get to know you?'. The approach outlined here will save you untold stress at networking meetings and social occasions as well as considerable time. We shall also explore the art of positioning and the role you seek with clients (hint: it may well need to change with each new client...). This is more powerful and in many ways far simpler than the old concept of a unique selling proposition (USP).

We shall spend some time on the mechanics of planning and running meetings so that you save time and gain the desired results more often. This approach can reduce the time needed to get to the point where you can ask for the engagement from three or four meetings to just one. The benefit is that you can spend more of your time on paid delivery as opposed to prospecting for clients.

This is also the start of a journey that allows you to be paid what you are worth rather than 'the market rate', whatever that may be. We look at fees and how to link the value you deliver to the cost of delivery so that the value is recognized by the client as far greater than the cost.

In the latter part of the book we look at the idea of strategic client leadership (as opposed to strategic account management). Not all clients can or should be treated strategically, no matter how large a part of your overall revenue they may be. We look at the process for selecting your strategic clients, how to work with them and the benefits (including locking out competitors and increasing price elasticity).

Lastly we look at the structure and systems that support your business. These allow you to work on your own business rather than owning your own job. It is not simply about IT systems (although IT is a great enabler of efficiency and effectiveness for your business if it is properly used). We look at building a systems mind-set and at the systems and processes that can help you to become as effective in running your business as you are when coaching clients.

Throughout the book we shall look at ways to minimize the impact of chance on your business in favour of predictability. One of the many benefits is to reduce the typical fluctuation of fee income that most coaches experience; the 'sine wave of poverty' as a friend of mine calls it. It also reduces stress and as most coaches know, it is anecdotally if not perhaps as yet clinically proven that 'stress makes you stupid'.

Let's take it as read that you possess the skills and characteristics of an excellent coach in your field. Success as a coach is then in finding and winning clients that you can coach successfully. Personal fulfilment and profitable fee revenue follow.

Let's begin...

The business of coaching: an overview

01

This is not a book about how to coach. It is a book about how one can make a reasonable income through coaching.

Coaching is something to which many individuals are attracted, sometimes after receiving coaching themselves, whether at work or privately. Having experienced the benefits of coaching and the impact it has had in their own lives, they feel an urge to do the same for others. Many undergo some form of training to become coaches in order to make a difference in the world and many of them will succeed in doing so. For some, the desire to make a difference does not lead to a wish to make a living from that work and they are content to coach free of charge or for very little money – enough to cover expenses. If you find yourself in this position, this book is not really intended for you, although it may help you in general terms to run other businesses.

The available statistics indicate that by no means all who seek to make an income from their coaching that allows them to pay the bills and make a living will do so. Those that are fortunate enough to have unearned income of some kind can obviously engage in coaching for the joy of it; for the sheer fulfilment of seeing the impact they can make with clients. Those with no other source of income often find that coaching must remain a spare time activity whilst they 'stick with the day job' to make ends meet. This book seeks to address that problem.

In responses to an online survey I carried out in the latter part of 2012, the single greatest challenge reported could be summarized as 'winning profitable clients'. Some called it 'marketing', others referred to 'building my network', others referred to 'finding buyers'. However it was phrased, the problem was similar – although interestingly nobody used the terms 'sales' or 'selling'. The aim of this book is to help you to overcome the client acquisition problem – to connect with more clients where there is a real personal and commercial fit and be paid a realistic fee for the value you deliver.

The coaching industry

A conventional approach to begin a book such as this would be to assess the market. However, there is no such thing as 'the coaching market': instead there are many coaching markets. Each has its own parameters that are typically defined by the types of client seeking to hire the coach and, perhaps of greater importance to coaches, each has its own spectrum of fee rates.

Commonly used distinctions include:

- executive coaching;
- business coaching;
- life coaching;
- career coaching;
- financial coaching;
- personal coaching;
- health and wellness coaching; and
- sports coaching.

These leave aside other disciplines that are often seen to be linked, such as counselling and mentoring, and potentially fields such as leadership development and some forms of consulting. Each discipline seeks to differentiate itself and to serve a different type of client. However, there are considerable areas of overlap and much interdisciplinary 'borrowing' of approaches and methodology. All of these disciplines share a number of common issues:

- fragmentation of the market place;

- a somewhat surprising lack of understanding among buyers of coaching (whether in roles such as HR professionals or as individual clients) of what coaching is and what could be realistic expectations of results;

- (at least to some degree) the lack of a commonly accepted set of standards, required qualifications or regulations across the field of coaching and multiple accreditation bodies, each with a somewhat different approach; and

- a large proportion of coaches making relatively little money from coaching (we explore this particular factor in more detail below).

This book focuses on only one of these factors: enabling you to become one of those coaches that does make a meaningful income from their coaching. However, we shall touch on the other issues because a willingness on the part of the coach to address them robustly with potential clients can act as a strong differentiator. In particular, we shall look at some ways in which you may be able to obviate the second issue (lack of understanding among buyers). However, the remaining items represent simply part of the context within which coaches operate today and are likely to do so for the foreseeable future, despite efforts to 'professionalize' the coaching markets generally.

Even if these other issues were to be resolved by the waving of some magic wand, the approaches that are outlined in this book will become no less relevant. Indeed, what is often presented as the levelling of the playing field in terms of qualification standards, accreditation, regulatory environment etc, removes a number of factors that some coaches elect to use today as differentiators even if they may be of limited relevance in the minds of clients. Your success need not depend on such things if you are able to use the approaches outlined in this book to:

- Identify the 'perfect' client for you.
- Locate and qualify such people so that they willingly enter a conversation with you. During that conversation, you can:
  - identify where there may be a commercial fit (by which I mean the opportunity for you to add significant value); and
  - learn what drives the client at an emotional level.

You will then be able to articulate a solution to the client's known problem in language that resonates with the listener.

Unless you are able to do all of those things consistently, you will find it harder to win business and there will be a tendency to 'force the fit'. That in turn means that you may end up accepting work where success is ill-defined (or even not able to be defined) and/or where there is a lack of shared values and behaviours. That will usually lead to disappointment for both you and the client. Sheer technical expertise as a coach – regardless of your chosen coaching discipline – will act as no more than a hygiene factor. It is not a differentiator. That is true especially in coaching, relative to other 'professional services', because the coaching relationship is so intensely personal. As we will explore later, it is a myth that clients buy coaching as such; they seek to resolve problems or to achieve aspirations or fulfil dreams. Coaching may be one of the approaches to be used but it need not be the only approach.

Some industry data...

Recognizing that coaching comprises a number of different disciplines, we can look at some overall numbers and trends. Interestingly, much of the available data is from periods prior to the onset of the financial market collapse and economic woes that began in 2008. The numbers are also somewhat inconsistent. That could be for many reasons and the aim here is not to offer a detailed analysis but to give some indications of scale and direction of travel.

I have added a list of resources available online at the end of this chapter in case you wish to develop a piece of collateral for your potential clients: something that indicates a potential return rate on coaching, for example. Be aware, however, that a fair amount of the 'evidence' is quite anecdotal and/or subjective. It would arguably not stand up to rigorous academic review although it is on the face of it quite compelling.

How many coaches?

In terms of the number of people working as coaches:

- the number of people working as life coaches in the United States was estimated at 10,000 by *Psychotherapy Networker* magazine (2008). However;
- a Markit Data report from 2007 put the total number of coaches working in the United States at 40,000 and the total fee income value of the industry at $2.4 billion, with an annual growth rate of around 18 per cent. It seems likely that the growth rate may have slowed. By contrast;
- the most recent International Coach Federation (ICF) survey (2012) estimates the number of coaches worldwide at around 48,000, although that number is an extrapolation.

Use of coaching

In terms of overall use of coaching:

- a 2011 UK survey by the Chartered Institute of Personnel and Development (CIPD) indicated that approximately three-quarters of companies that responded used coaching (although this represented a decline from the 90 per cent level indicated in 2009);

- of those companies that continued to use coaching, 84 per cent were using it to a greater degree than in the past;

- where coaching was used, the percentage of work done by external coaches (as opposed to in-house) had increased from 14 per cent to 20 per cent;

- almost half of all respondents in 2011 said that coaching was used as a tool for performance improvement versus only around 25 per cent in 2009.

Clearly the above relates mostly to business or executive coaching. There seems to be little in the way of collated data on usage for disciplines such as life coaching.

Fees and workload

As for the fees charged by coaches and their workload, the figures vary widely depending on the nature of the coaching in question. For example:

- A *Harvard Business Review* survey carried out in 2009 indicated that the average fee among the 100 or so business coaches that responded to their questionnaire was $500 per hour or equivalent (similar to the rate for a psychologist in Manhattan or a Wall Street lawyer).

- By contrast, the Association for Coaching found in 2004 that hourly rates for some 43 per cent of respondents to its survey (apparently mainly life coaches) were in the range £50–£75 per hour (roughly $90–$135 at the time...).

- Just under half of all coaches see two clients or fewer per week on average according to a 2006 survey by CoachStart (a coach training firm). The same survey found that, for a similar proportion of respondents, their major challenge was filling their practice – ie finding clients and winning business.

- The data in the following tables are taken from the book by Anne Scoular, *The FT Guide to Business Coaching* (FT Prentice Hall, 2011) and give an indication of fee levels and personal income levels for approximately 400 business coaches, based on data from 2009.

TABLE 1.1 How much have you personally billed your clients in total for coaching services in the past 12 months?

Billing band	Percentage of respondents
Under £5,000	25.5
£5,001–£10,000	11.8
£10,001–£30,000	23.0
£30,001–£50,000	12.7
£50,001–£75,000	5.4
£75,001–£100,000	6.9
£100,001–£150,000	3.9
£150,001–£200,000	2.5
£200,001–£250,000	0.7
Over £250,000	0.7
Not known/Not applicable	6.9

NOTE: based on the above data, over 60 per cent of the respondents billed £30,000 or less for coaching in the previous year. See also Table 1.3 below.

TABLE 1.2   What was your personal income from coaching services in the past 12 months?

Income band	Percentage of respondents
Under £5,000	22.9
£5,001–£10,000	13.3
£10,001–£30,000	22.7
£30,001–£50,000	13.3
£50,001–£75,000	9.4
£75,001–£100,000	5.9
£100,001–£150,000	2.7
£150,001–£200,000	1.0
Not known/Not applicable	8.9

NOTE: The words 'from coaching services' above are underlined for emphasis. It would appear that many coaches (especially those that earn higher levels of income) derive at least some income from activities other than coaching as such.

This represents a relatively small sample but the distribution pattern is clear. A few coaches make a fair amount of money but most make an income from coaching at the 'paying hobby' level, which is likely to be supplemented by other activities. The ICF Survey from 2012 indicates that the median income for coaches worldwide, on a 'purchasing power parity' basis (ie adjusted for exchange rates and also local buying power), was approximately equivalent to $25,000 per annum (roughly £15,500 equivalent at the time of writing). In other words, 50 per cent of all coaches make less than that figure. The approaches outlined in this book aim to overcome that problem.

TABLE 1.3 Please allocate your approximate annual income split to the activities listed below

Area of activity	Percentage income split
Coaching	34.3
Training/development/facilitation	23.8
Consulting	19.6
Employed part time	3.7
Work in academic institution	1.9
Mentoring	1.4
Non-executive director	1.1
Interim roles	1.0
Research services	0.3
Other	12.9

Overall:

- It looks as though the numbers of people engaged in coaching are increasing.
- A small proportion of coaches do well from coaching whilst the majority make relatively little money.
- Fee levels for coaching vary widely, with those working in the business/executive coaching field being far higher than those in the life coaching/individual coaching field.

- It is not clear that fee levels across all fields of coaching have kept up with inflation over the five years from 2007 (the start of the financial crisis). Anecdotally they appear to have fallen somewhat in absolute terms in the business coaching world. However, in absolute terms fees for life coaching may well have been maintained even if (a) they have not kept pace with inflation; and (b) they start from a lower base.

What do we mean by 'coaching?'

As mentioned above, what constitutes coaching does not seem typically to be well-understood by either buyers or end clients. There is a sense that people 'know it when they see it' but find it hard to define. Many coaches think in terms of a 'non-directive' approach as the hallmark of coaching, as opposed to mentoring for example. For some the boundaries between coaching and psychotherapy on the one hand and mentoring on the other are hazy. There are significant differences in the definition of coaching between some of the main authorities on the subject.

John Whitmore (1996) defined it with admirable simplicity as: 'Unlocking a person's potential to maximise their own performance.' Other definitions include:

- 'Primarily a short-term intervention aimed at performance improvement or developing a particular competence' (Clutterbuck, 2003); and
- 'A collaborative, solution-focused, results-oriented and systematic process in which the coach facilitates the enhancement of work performance, life experience, self-directed learning and personal growth of the coachee' (Grant, 2003).

It appears that many, if not all, of those who make a good income from coaching do not limit themselves to coaching alone as their source of income, however. Many will also undertake consulting work, mentoring and roles such as non-executive directorships and interim management jobs; all as parts of a portfolio career.

I certainly follow that approach and indeed in the context of a coaching engagement will 'float' to where the client needs help, rather than limiting myself to coaching alone. I firmly believe that the client does not buy coaching but instead the delivery of results. Coaching is a tool that I use when appropriate but it is by no means the only one. In other words coaching is something that I do. It does not define what I 'am' to my clients. It seems to me that anyone contemplating running a business as a coach should consider carefully how 'purist' they wish to be in coaching and recognize the potential impact their decision may have on their ability to generate income, even if it may in theory provide a far clearer positioning message to potential clients.

Who buys coaching?

The actual buying process for coaching seems to depend on the nature of the coaching sought. However, in the vast majority of cases, the final decision on coach selection seems to rest with the end client or coachee. In the case of business/executive coaching, an initial shortlist section may well be made by the HR or learning and development (L&D) department of the organization. However the final choice will usually depend on the personal chemistry between the coach and the end client combined with trust that the desired results can be delivered.

In some cases, that may lead to the choice of a coach with an approach that is perceived to be 'softer' or 'gentler': it is quite rare in my experience for clients to seek actively to be challenged. That can lead to slower delivery of results or indeed to undershooting on delivery, but my experience indicates that coaching is such a personal and intense relationship that it is usually best for the client to select the person they feel best able to work with. It may prove necessary to transfer to another coach after a period of time when the client is able to take advantage of a different, perhaps 'tougher' approach.

In the case of life coaching, career coaching and personal coaching, the selection may well be made by the end client with no formal external input. Choice may be based on referrals or in some cases search engine results followed by website review and a phone call that may then lead to a chemistry meeting. That being so, the need for you to have an adequate website that acts as a tool to attract clients is clear (and we look at this in Chapters 3 and 4). In some cases the client may rely simply on a referral as long as the personal chemistry is adequate.

This sort of imprecision in business/executive and life coaching is almost certainly a product of the fact that there is limited regulation of such coaching and little by way of agreed accreditation factors. In other words it is hard for buyers to form a view of coaches and their capabilities, based on a common and consistent set of objective criteria. Individual coaches therefore have an opportunity to use this situation to their advantage in differentiating themselves from possible competitors. In other words, if you have undergone accredited training for example (whether or not you have chosen to become certified) that can act as a 'tick in the box' for some buyers. We shall look at other differentiating factors and how to articulate them in subsequent chapters.

Coach matching/broking services

Recognizing that the greatest single problem that most coaches seem to have is client acquisition (ie marketing, selling and winning new business), and that buyers of coaching can find the selection process daunting, a number of coach 'brokerages' or 'matching services' have grown up. Examples include TXG: **www.txgltd.com** and CoachMatch: **www.coachmatch.co.uk**. These organizations work almost entirely in the business/executive coaching field; indeed I am not aware of one that works in other fields. From the point of view of the coach, these firms do much of the hard work of winning and managing relationships with client firms. They are often quite selective in their choice of coaches and it will usually be necessary for the coach to have had formal training via an accredited course in order to be selected, even if they do not always insist on individual certification.

Approval to go onto the panel of some of these firms is something of an accolade and proof that you have a good degree of credibility as a coach, so it should be a boost to self-confidence. If that is the case, one might (churlishly, perhaps) ask why you do not use that credibility and self-confidence to secure your own work. That question is germane because the brokerage is paid (typically) by way of a significant percentage of the chosen coach's fee; often equivalent to that payable to a head-hunter for recruitment – say, north of 25 per cent. That fee share may be a one-off but can be for all time. This book will provide a toolkit that should enable you to win your own work if you choose or to use broking services selectively if it makes sense; in other words by choice rather than by default.

For the buyer of coaching, the use of a coach matching service can offer a level of comfort based on the rigour of the selection process and save time on shortlisting. They also get to access coaches they might not otherwise see. It is akin to the use of a recruitment agency as opposed to relying on one's personal network or a press advertisement to fill a high-level job vacancy. Some of the brokerages also carry out a quality assurance (QA) process during and after a coaching engagement. Again this is sold as a great benefit to the client firm. It is a practice that independent coaches may do well to follow as part of their ongoing client retention work (which we look at in Chapters 8 and 10).

Coach selection processes and certification

A considerable amount of work has been carried out by organizations such as CIPD in the United Kingdom to offer a framework for coach selection. Their very useful guide to coaching and buying coaching services can be downloaded as a pdf file from their website,

www.cipd.co.uk. If nothing else it is helpful to understand how some buyers will approach coach selection. Books such as *Pinpointing Excellence: The Key to Finding a Quality Executive Coach* by Dr John Reed (published by Bright Sky Press, 2011) seek to put forward a robust basis for the selection of coaches and also to move towards the creation of a level playing field in terms of regulatory environment etc.

However, my experience indicates that the selection process for many coaching assignments can still best be described as 'loose', at the time of writing; at least in the United Kingdom, and that has remained the case for over a decade. It would, however, be naïve to expect this to remain so indefinitely and it does seem that changes are afoot with a greater emphasis on certification as a selection factor among business coaches. In the United States it appears that certification is a greater issue both for business/executive coaches and in the life coaching/personal coaching sphere. That may be the result of a more litigious environment or for several other reasons.

An exception to this highly flexible approach to the buying of coaching in the United Kingdom is the field of sports coaching. Here, the whole accreditation/qualification procedure is typically far more rigorous than in the field of business or executive coaching, let alone life coaching. In the United Kingdom, sports coaches are trained in accordance with a framework set up by Sport UK that applies across all sports. Within each sport, the detailed standards are adjusted to ensure relevance to the sport, but coaches are classified according to Levels 1–4, with 1 being a sound, basic level that will allow the individual to coach safely under supervision. Level 2 is appropriate for those seeking to undertake paid coaching work at club level and indeed it is a health and safety requirement that a Level 2 coach is present at any club training session in order that the activity is covered by the relevant sport's insurance scheme. Level 3 is required for national and premier level coaching and Level 4 represents a coach qualified to work at international level. Very few coaches progress to Levels 3 and 4, partly due to the rigour of the qualification syllabus and partly due to lack of available courses.

In this instance, buyers are able to shortlist coaches based on a combination of standardized qualification and referral/reputation, with the personal or group chemistry only then coming into play. However, although a given sports coach may have relevant qualifications this does not necessarily evidence ability or depth of expertise, nor does it evidence the capacity to engage those being coached effectively. The same is of course true in respect of certification in other fields of coaching.

At first sight, it is odd that sports coaching appears to be so much better organized and regulated given the potential for significant long-term impact delivered by other forms of coaching. However, in sports coaching there is the risk of physical injury if coaching is carried out improperly; something less likely to occur in the context of, say, life coaching. In a 'health and safety' driven and increasingly litigious culture, the need for adequate training in a situation where physical injury can occur seems perhaps more obvious. The issue of flexible buying of coaching does of course create opportunities for providers of coaching who can differentiate themselves through robust certification.

Factors that influence the buying process

The way in which coaching is bought differs depending on a combination of:

- the nature of the end client and the issues they seek to address
- the type of coaching (eg business vs life); and
- (in the case of corporate/business/executive coaching) the nature of the organization.

In many – arguably most – cases, expertise on the part of the coach is assumed. In other words if you call yourself a coach and give the perception that you know how to coach and perhaps understand something of psychology and tools such as neuro-linguistic programming (NLP), no deeper investigation will be carried out. Able coaches who have gained formal qualifications can of course use these as differentiators to a degree. However, although your qualifications may allow you access to a given client, that is only the start of winning an assignment.

Where you are looking to engage directly with the end client, regardless of the type of coaching you offer, the initial approach will usually be made by the client to you, based on a specific referral, search engine results, some form of directory or other listing or word of mouth. It is of course also possible that you will meet socially, at a venue such as a conference or seminar or at a specific 'business networking' meeting. The client will typically be looking for a combination of:

- good personal chemistry/rapport;
- a clear understanding of what you do, the type of client that you prefer to work with and the benefits you deliver;
- comfort that you understand both the issues to be addressed and the client's view of their own situation/capabilities;
- (assuming that the first three are positive), some form of reference or social proof/testimonials. That may include verification that you have formal training as a coach but by no means always does.

In later chapters we explore how to manage these initial contacts so that you maximize the likelihood of winning work with clients that you want to work with. It is important that you give yourself permission to be at least as careful in selecting your clients as they are in selecting you.

In business/executive coaching it is far more likely that the engagement will come about through a complex sale process; complex in that more than one buyer is involved and each will need a somewhat different approach. Again we explore this in more detail in subsequent chapters. The larger the organization, the more likely it is that the HR/L&D department will be involved in initial coach selection and the development of a shortlist. That may be with a view to shortlisting a coach for a particular individual or with a view to creating or reassessing a panel of coaches. That panel may be used in conjunction with in-house coaches.

CIPD data indicate that the percentage of coaching carried out by in-house coaches has become somewhat lower between 2009 and 2011 and this might be due to perceptions that an external professional can achieve more in some cases than an in-house coach. Again each implies a different approach. However, it may be helpful to have in mind that your competition as an independent is not necessarily other independent coaches but the in-house coach. Consider the way that you discuss the value you add accordingly. Simply 'knocking' competition from whatever source is of course poor practice and usually counterproductive.

It is quite likely that an L&D/HR professional will seek to use some sort of set selection criteria for their coaches and that this may include evidence of accredited training if not individual certification. If you are not individually certified, you may be asked to describe the ethical standards to which you adhere. (It would be wise both to prepare for that question and to ensure that your description of your ethical policies is at least equivalent to those of one or other of the bodies offering certification.) It is also more likely that you as a coach will approach such L&D/HR professionals rather than them approaching you, unless it is by way of a referral. This changes the game completely and takes it to another level involving far more rigorous preparation and the need to be well informed about the client firm and the potential opportunities for you to add significant value. You will need to be able to articulate specifically what that value-add may be and tailor your description so that it touches the specific needs of the client firm and of the individual. Hence the need to gather information rather than simply making a presentation (something we look at in Chapters 4 and 5).

In some very large organizations – and quite frequently in public sector organizations – coaching is treated just like any other procurement activity. You can expect to receive a Request For Proposal (RFP), which may be a lengthy document. That will typically be followed by a series of interviews and/or a panel interview. There may well also be an assessment centre that includes such things as observed roleplay coaching. If you pass these various tests you may find yourself added to a list of coaches approved by the organization. However, that in itself is no guarantee of work, nor is it an indication that the fee levels will be as high as you might expect or hope.

Beware the RFP! In 2009 I was asked to submit an RFP for coaching work with senior medical consultants working in the NHS. The RFP was 42 pages in length and required (among other things) three specific client references. That would have been difficult since my usual contract with clients includes a clause forbidding the seeking of references from them (on grounds of confidentiality) and the use of their name or that of their firm in my own marketing. Had I been approved following the RFP, I would have undergone two sets of interviews on different days in a distant location and then an assessment centre some two to three weeks later at another distant location.

The whole process would have taken some four days of my time. If successful at that assessment centre I would have been on an approved list of coaches that could be selected for work at a fee rate that was roughly one third of my usual one. I decided not to complete the RFP: the time commitment would have been too great for no certainty of a paid engagement, even had the fee rate on offer been acceptable.

How do coaching businesses operate?

Leaving aside the large number of coaches that operate in-house (ie within firms and organizations where they are employees), the majority of independent coaches operate as individuals. For that reason much of this book focuses on such individuals. However, the approaches apply equally to any form of coaching business (and indeed far more widely). There are groups of coaches (for example The Alliance: **www.alliancecoaching.co.uk**) and a few full-blown 'corporate' entities (such as Praesta: **www.praesta.com**) and franchises such as ActionCoach® (**www.actioncoach.com**). Many more work in loose groups of 'associates'. This seems not to depend on the nature of the coaching offered or the type of client. We examine the various business models in more detail in Chapter 9.

It may be tempting to view a group of associates as akin to a partnership. It is not. You can choose to work with an associate or not – pretty much at will. With a partner you are accepting, implicitly or explicitly, liability for actions taken by your partner. Even if you do not have a formal partnership arrangement but allow yourself to be spoken of as a partner, it sets perceptions in the minds of others and in particular of potential clients. If a client likes and trusts you but has a visceral dislike of someone who talks of you as a business partner, that dislike will rub off on you. It is for good reason that a friend of mine has a firm policy that she will have employees and contractors (even sub-contractors on occasion) but not partners in her business. I tend to follow the same approach.

If you do decide to go down the route of partnership, the basis of your partnership agreement must be written down and signed by each partner. Among other things that agreement must cover:

- ownership of any existing client relationships;
- the basis of fee splits and/or income division;
- contributions by individuals to the business and the basis of repayment; and
- a mechanism to dissolve the partnership and events that will trigger dissolution automatically.

We look at this in more detail in Chapter 9. In my experience the number of actual partnerships in the various fields of coaching is relatively small compared to the number of groups operating as associates.

Whether as a partnership or as a group of associates the key skill is not usually coaching but client acquisition. Coaching is in fact, more often than not, the pleasurable outcome of the hard work of marketing and selling. In this book we shall look at ways to change that balance so that your hit rate in your sales meetings is increased and the time taken to arrive at the point where the client is able to say 'yes' is minimized. The result can be more time spent on actual coaching, if that is what you want. Remember, the CoachStart survey referred to above found that roughly three-quarters of respondents saw five clients or fewer per week and almost half saw two or fewer.

How is coaching carried out?

In terms of the mechanics of how coaches work, the majority appear to work 1:1 and face to face. That may be changing as tools such as Skype (**www.skype.com**) and GoToMeeting (**www.gotomeeting.co.uk**) allow reasonably good and also low cost or free conference calling facilities, with or without video, to work both remotely and with groups. I am aware of several business coaches in the United States who work increasingly with groups because it allows them to attract a greater number of clients who have limited budgets.

By combining these clients into groups (which may be three to five in number, but sometimes far more) the client can experience coaching and gain good value for a relatively low fee. The coach may in fact make more money per hour coaching a group than would be possible working 1:1. That said, group coaching is not an easy option. Also the means of marketing and selling group coaching may differ from the norm with a greater reliance on direct marketing and advertising.

I have done group coaching on occasion (within client firms) and acknowledge that it can be beneficial for the clients, especially those who prefer to 'hide' in a group, are inherently shy, or may not be ready as yet for a 1:1 deep dive into issues that may be uncomfortable for them. I found that the coaching was not usually as deep or impactful, however and hence less rewarding to me. I also found that there was demand from group members to move to 1:1 coaching after a handful of group sessions. It can, however, be a great way to develop or to extend a coaching practice and the fact that you offer group coaching can confer added credibility in some cases. It also allows you to offer a greater variety of pricing points to clients. That is beneficial especially where an individual seeks a 'taster' with low financial risk to themselves.

How much money do coaches make?

Once again, as outlined above, fee rates vary depending on the type of coaching, the nature of the client and the experience (and indeed self-confidence!) of the coach. In the same way as there is no such thing as a single coaching market, there is no such thing as a single 'market rate'. The actual levels of fee vary widely, as does the basis of charging. We look at fee setting in some detail in Chapter 7. I put forward the idea that there is no such thing as a 'market rate', whether for coaching as a whole or for any given field of coaching. We also explore various different ways to set your fee, other than the default 'hourly rate'. (I recommend you avoid the hourly rate approach if possible: you may need to work out an hourly rate to ensure that your work is profitable and that you can make enough to pay your bills, but I prefer a retainer fee or a 'rate for the job' approach.)

Predictably the higher levels of overall income (and also of hourly fee rates) have long been and apparently remain in business/executive coaching. Even here, however, not many coaches make an income that is much above national average wages for manual work. We have to assume that they don't do it for the money alone but for the fulfilment that coaching gives them. The tools and approaches outlined in this book can help you to change that balance in favour of your bank account, however.

The business case for coaching

Why do clients buy coaching? Simplistically, because it works! The issue is, how do we know that? Sadly, the volume of data to prove that point is relatively limited although the anecdotal evidence is clear and seems to tally with common sense. There seems to be a considerable amount of data on the impact of coaching in the field of sports. It is by no means coincidental that top athletes universally use coaching to improve their performance. The differences in performances can be measured quite simply in many cases: a consistent improvement in lap times or distance a discus is thrown for example.

A small number of investigations suggest a return on investment (ROI) of between 5.5 and 7.9 times for executive coaching, combined with a variety of 'soft' benefits including

- working relationships with direct reports (reported by 77 per cent of executives);
- working relationships with immediate supervisors (71 per cent);
- teamwork (67 per cent);
- working relationships with peers (63 per cent);
- job satisfaction (61 per cent);
- conflict reduction (52 per cent);
- organizational commitment (44 per cent); and
- working relationships with clients (37 per cent).

(These figures appear in a study by the Manchester Consulting Group in 2001, which is often cited as a definitive case for coaching.) An internal report of the Personnel Management Association showed that when training is combined with coaching, individuals increase their productivity by an average of 80 per cent compared to 22 per cent with training alone. The ICF in a recent press advertisement, quoting data from their own surveys, indicated a performance improvement of 82 per cent through coaching. Clearly these examples come from the field of business/executive coaching, where one might reasonably expect that it is more likely for concrete and measurable results to be sought and indeed measured. It appears, however, that this is by no means always the case and it is interesting to note that the measurement of the impact of coaching or even the achievement of desired results is not always enforced even in a corporate environment. In many such cases, the 'measurement' of results is largely anecdotal and based on improvements reported by coachees. Where bottom line results are seen to improve, for example, it is likely that coaching has had an impact but it may not be the sole factor involved.

Even where the impact of coaching is measured by the use of instruments such as 360-degree reviews, it is hard to avoid the effect of subjective views. It is also arguable that the direct link between coaching and improved performance is hard to prove as there can be multiple other factors involved. The study by Dr David Peterson presented at the ICF conference at San Diego in 2011 (see references on page 30) outlines the problems of assessing the ROI of coaching very succinctly, whilst acknowledging that the broad indication of positive results is compelling.

However, the 2011 survey by CIPD entitled The Coaching Climate (**www.cipd.co.uk** › HR Resources › Survey Reports) indicates that coaching is used in the corporate environment mainly as a tool for performance enhancement. In the corporate context, there are two further issues to consider:

- In many businesses, over half of coaching is carried out by line managers and by in-house as opposed to external coaches. It is not clear whether the expectations of work with an external coach differ from those of working with an in-house coach.

- If a coachee is paired with an in-house coach, it is likely that the coach will be a reasonably senior individual with direct and perhaps long-term experience in the business. It is possible that they both see the relationship as mentoring rather than coaching, (eg directive versus non-directive) and act accordingly.

Last but by no means least I have come across executives who have agreed to (or sought to buy) coaching when what was in fact needed was a highly focused consulting approach to handle a specific problem. As one client said to me in 2008 at the height of the financial crisis, 'Stephen, I don't have time to be coached. I just need your help to survive right now. Tell me what to do!' When you first meet a client it will be important to ensure that you both understand the term 'coaching' in the same way in order to manage expectations appropriately.

But we get ahead of ourselves. For now, let's turn in Chapter 2 to identifying the right kind of client for you in terms of both the personal and the commercial fit for you to work together.

CHAPTER SUMMARY

- Relatively few coaches make significant income from coaching – at least not from coaching alone. Recent ICF survey data indicates median income from coaching, worldwide, on a 'purchasing power parity' basis, is around $25,000 per annum: ie half of all coaches make less than that figure. By contrast a 2009 survey of business coaches indicates that approximately 4 per cent of them earn over £100k per annum.

- Those coaches that earn the higher levels of income tend to work in a business/executive coaching role and also to offer additional services such as mentoring, training and consultancy. They also tend to have a robust commercial focus on their business.

- The coaching 'industry' is fragmented with multiple accreditation bodies, no real objective criteria for coach selection, limited regulation and with many buyers who have limited expertise in coaching and indeed for whom the definition of what coaching 'is' is not entirely clear. However, they do recognize that clients buy results.

- Coaching businesses tend to operate in the form of individuals who act as freelancers/independents. However, some groups of associates exist and are successful. There are one or two quasi-corporate coaching firms such as Praesta and some franchise operations such as Action Coach. Increasing numbers of companies and professional firms are developing and using in-house coaches.

- Coaching is typically carried out face to face and 1:1. However, this model is changing as coaches use technology to coach remotely (eg Skype, telephone, video-conference) and encourage clients to work in groups in order to make fees affordable for each individual client and maximize revenue per unit of time for the coach.

- The business case for coaching is intuitively compelling although the evidence is often anecdotal and/or somewhat subjective. Part of the problem in producing objective evidence appears to be the lack of a clear definition of success prior to coaching and rigorous measurement of the relevant factors before and after coaching. In some cases, it can be hard to isolate the impact of coaching from other factors.

References

The following list of reference material concerning the 'benefits of coaching/a business case for coaching/ROI of coaching' is set out in no particular order, either in terms of date produced or of perceived value. Each item can be found online; most of it can be accessed free of charge, but some must be purchased.

To my mind, the evidence that coaching delivers significant benefit is compelling. However, that evidence is somewhat inconsistent in terms of specific results and also in terms of the method of assessment:

a point made in detail in the material produced by Dr David Peterson in the second item listed below.

ICF, Global Coaching Study 2012

Executive Coaching: A Critical Review of the Research. David B Peterson, PhD, Google, Inc

I/O-OB Conference, 6 March 2011, San Diego, CA

'The Case for Executive Coaching', by Pamela S Wise, PhD and Laurie S Voss, PhD, a paper by the Lore Research Institute 2002

International Coaching Psychology Review, Vol 5, No 1, March 2010 (Published by the British Psychological Society and the Australian Psychological Society)

International Coaching Psychology Review, Vol 2, No 2, July 2007 (Published by the British Psychological Society and the Australian Psychological Society)

'Business Impact of Executive Coaching: Results of a study by Manchester, Inc' (Published in the Proceedings of the ICF Annual Conference, August 2001)

'Maximizing the Impact of Executive Coaching: Behavioural Change, Organizational Outcomes, and Return on Investment', by Joy McGovern, PhD, Michael Lindemann, PhD, Monica Vergara, MA, Stacey Murphy, Linda Barker, MA, and Rodney Warrenfeltz, PhD. Published in *The Manchester Review*, 2001, Vol 6, No 1

'What ROI Studies of Executive Coaching Tell Us', by Merrill C. Anderson PhD, CEO of Metrix Global LLC © Linkage 2004–08

'Calculating the ROI of Coaching', by Stephanie Sparrow. This article first appeared in *Training and Coaching Today*: **www.personneltoday.com**

'Executive Coaching Project, Evaluation of Findings', a study conducted by Harder & Company for Compass Point Non-Profit Services, September 2003

Individual Diversity and Psychology in Organizations, edited by MJ Davidson and SL Fielden, Hoboken, John Wiley & Sons

Techniques for Coaching and Mentoring, (David Clutterbuck with David Megginson), 2005, Elsevier Butterworth Heinemann

Solution Focused Coaching – Managing People in a Complex World, Antony M Grant, Pearson Education 2003

Coaching For Performance: Growing People, Performance and Purpose, John Whitmore, Nicholas Brealey Publishing, 2002

Identifying the right clients

02

Coaching or a coach?

I consider the term 'coach' to be a verb not a noun; in other words it is something I do rather than something I am – I coach but I am not only a coach. Coaching is just a tool used to deliver results to clients. Where appropriate, in order to deliver the results required by the clients, mentoring and/or consulting approaches may also be appropriate. I make it clear to the client in what role I seek to act and when it changes (which may occur more than once during a session). This is simply part of the contracting process and the client may decide whether they wish me to act in a particular role or not. It is, after all, their engagement not mine. However, where it becomes clear that coaching alone will not deliver the required result, the client will need to agree how to proceed.

In my experience, clients tend to be far more concerned about achieving results than they are about the process by which these results are achieved. Indeed I would go as far as to say that clients rarely – if ever – buy coaching as such: they buy results in the form of problem resolution or ability to fulfil dreams or achieve aspirations.

This does of course beg a somewhat existential question about what you are – or seek to be – as a coach. Some would no doubt argue that one can either be a coach or one can be something else (mentor, consultant etc) but not both at almost the same time. Whilst this is a real issue for many coaches, it seems to me that coaching is simply one of several developmental tools that can be used to help a client and sits along a continuum of such tools rather than apart from them.

I confess that I prefer to coach a client where coaching is practicable and I feel it is the appropriate tool, because I believe that it is most effective in cementing behavioural change over the long term. In many cases the degree of positive impact that can be achieved is far greater through coaching than by way of other approaches, some of which can be thought of by the client as outsourcing the problem; hence reducing ownership of the need for change and for action to effect change.

However, especially over the years since the financial crisis that started in 2008, many clients, both new and long-standing, have said at one point something along the lines of: 'Stephen, I don't have time to be coached; I need you to tell me what I need to do in order to survive right now.' That is probably not a good moment to have a debate about the relative merits of a coaching approach because the client is simply not ready to engage in it.

The importance of positioning

In this chapter, we look at the combination of the role in which you seek to position yourself (coach, consultant, mentor, solutions provider, teller of truth as you see it...) and the types of client with whom you prefer to work. This is a piece of strategic marketing in miniature. It offers three distinct benefits:

1 You will be able to identify the type of client with whom you can be most successful and with whom you are most likely to enjoy working. As part of that process you will explore the value you are able to deliver so that you can focus on those clients where you can make the greatest difference – surely the aspiration of the vast majority of coaches.

2 You will be better able to define the type of referral that you would most like to receive. The two are of course closely linked and we look in more detail at referrals in Chapter 3.

3 If you can define clearly the type of client with whom you wish to work and the factors that will allow you credibly to approach that type of client, you minimize the probability of summary rejection and maximize the likelihood of winning business once you meet the potential client. The result is that you save time and effort.

Many coaches believe that they are able to coach literally anyone successfully. In theory that may be possible. However, experience indicates that it is rarely the case in practice. Separately, in the mind of the client your coaching credentials are only one element in the hiring decision – and often a fairly small one. Factors such as personal chemistry and relevant experience often carry more weight, not least because relatively few clients have any objective means to judge your ability as a coach and the whole field of training and certification is confused and fragmented (as outlined in Chapter 1). If the client perceives relevant experience to be a key selection factor for their coach, no amount of positive references and testimonials will overcome that perception and if you lack that experience, the chance of being hired is slender.

There are of course two sides to this equation: how the client experiences you and the value you deliver for them and how you experience the client and feel that you will enjoy working with them (or not as the case may be). In an ideal world, both sides would be equally positive and indeed it is often the case that, as a coach, you will gain as much satisfaction and joy from a manifestly successful engagement as the client does. The converse is also usually true: if the client is dissatisfied with the results of an engagement and the personal chemistry is less than happy, both parties will feel negative to some degree. In some engagements, where the results for the client were objectively excellent I have elected not to work with that individual in the future. The vast majority of those situations arise because of some dissonance of values and behaviours. For example,

I elect not to work with those I perceive to be bullies or those who appear to me to be habitual liars or unduly prone to exaggeration. I know other excellent coaches who are willing to do so and I would prefer to refer the client to one or other of them rather than fight that dissonance: life is simply too short to do otherwise.

You may prefer, as a rule, not to undertake purely remedial work but may do so where you believe that you can deliver outstanding results for the client; partly because the client recognizes the need for change and for help in making that change. If it becomes clear that a client does not want to make the changes agreed or is unwilling to 'do the work', you may find it hard to renew such an engagement and in some cases, following a discussion, will agree an early termination (with an appropriate refund of fees if necessary).

In order to develop a coaching practice that is successful for you as well as for your clients, I therefore recommend that you decide early on what factors define a 'perfect' client for you and what would cause you to decline an engagement. Especially in the early days of building your coaching practice, it can be tempting to take on any engagement that promises to provide income, on the assumption that any revenue is better than no revenue and that all revenue is the same. Experience indicates that neither is the case.

What makes the client 'right'?

Most coaches enter the world of coaching because they have a desire to 'make a difference' or to 'enable clients to realize their potential' or something similar. Relatively few become coaches simply to increase their personal income (and indeed this is reflected in the available data on income derived from coaching). If one accepts that income is an outcome of success and that one can be far more successful in coaching certain types of client (and the type of client differs from person to person) then surely it makes sense to spend a little time identifying the types of client where you can be most successful. The benefit is not only to deliver maximum value to the client (which in turn is more likely to result in positive referrals) but also to gain maximum satisfaction for yourself from seeing the results of your coaching.

Identifying the 'right' clients for you is a form of strategic marketing and positioning that combines:

- the definition of your 'perfect' client (no, that will not be simply 'anyone with a credit card');
- the 'pain' that the 'perfect' client is likely to experience or the 'dream' that they seek to fulfil;
- your personal brand and values;
- your personal journey to date and the experience you have gained both personally and professionally; and
- the benefits that you deliver (as opposed to the process by which you deliver them).

In identifying the right clients for you, you will also be able to visualize the role that you seek to play for those clients and how you would like them to see and to experience you; what you will 'be' for them. The result is that you will be able to see more easily where there may be a 'commercial fit' for you to work with a given potential client so that you can more easily answer the question 'Why should I hire you?'

Separately, as mentioned above, the more closely you can define your perfect client, the easier it becomes to define what a great referral looks like for you. In addition, the more clearly you can define a 'good' client for you, the less time you will waste on 'meeting to meet' in order to chase any engagement that might be possible rather than targeting those where you can be most successful.

We look at time allocation in Chapter 9. Suffice it to say here that time is your single most important asset. Money can be borrowed; time cannot, nor can it be recycled. Once an hour has been used it cannot be regained or re-used. The only way in which time can be leveraged is to outsource elements of your business or to hire employees or contractors. These can be very useful approaches – indeed they may become mandatory as your practice develops – but only as and when there is sufficient revenue to justify them.

Identifying the right client

Start with what won't work for you. Especially for those new to coaching, it may be quite hard to visualize what a 'good' client looks like. It may in fact be easier to start by defining what it is not. Experience indicates that some of the best value in any business is in deciding what not to do, not least because it reduces the number of variables or dead-ends. There is now some research that indicates that human beings are happier with the choices they make if the number of available options is smaller. I recommend starting by thinking about your answers to the question 'What characteristics and behaviours on the part of a client would make me unhappy or irritate me?'

Answers could include basic items such as:

- being abrasive;
- use of bad language;
- anger;
- failing to turn up for meetings or arriving late;
- failing to pay fees or paying late;
- poor personal chemistry with you;
- lack of a real 'fit' (commercially or personally);
- unwillingness/inability to set clear goals and define success;
- failure to make changes or to carry out tasks that have been agreed (I think of this as 'not keeping their side of the bargain').

It will quickly become clear that many if not all of these items are in fact under your control and can be addressed as part of your initial contracting and goal-setting conversations with the client. The key, however, is to identify those values or behaviours 'up with which

I will not put' (as Winston Churchill famously said). If you can avoid those behaviours that you find truly toxic it becomes easier to handle most other issues.

In addition to the 'values and behaviours' that you prefer not to encounter, you may also want to add factors that encompass, for example, their position in a corporate hierarchy (in the case of business or executive coaches in particular but perhaps for others); the sort of work they do or even factors such as political affiliation, to the extent that these are important to you.

I was once asked to meet a potential client who was the founder and chief executive of an IT consultancy that had grown very rapidly over a fairly short time. He was now keen to be able to step back somewhat and to feel that he could delegate day-to-day management of the business in order to devote more time to sailing his yacht in the Mediterranean. He wanted some help with that transition. It sounded like a very interesting engagement.

The HR director who set up the meeting emphasized that the CEO set great store by ethics in his business. I should have investigated more thoroughly what that actually meant. As is so often the case, assumption is the mother of all errors. During the first few minutes of our meeting, the CEO went into some detail about the fact that he was rabidly anti-smoking and drinking and was a convinced pacifist. His firm therefore refused to do business with any defence contractor or with the Defence Ministry; ditto any company involved in the 'twin evils' of tobacco and alcohol. I responded that it was unlikely, on that basis, that we could work successfully together given that I was a former military officer who enjoyed a glass of wine and had been known on occasion in my schooldays to take an illicit drag behind the bicycle shed. The lesson from this situation is of course not only that it is necessary to decide what a 'good' (and indeed a 'bad') client might look like for you but to be sure to ask questions so that you have a good idea where any given prospective client sits along that continuum.

What does 'good' look like for you?

Having thought briefly about the factors that might define a 'poor' client for you, it is time to look at how to define a good – better yet a 'great' – client for you. The factors that you choose will vary depending on the nature of your chosen branch of coaching and of course your own personal preferences and prior experience. No potential client is likely to be a perfect match with your criteria so you will of course need to determine where the boundary of 'acceptable' lies. This exercise helps you to define the 'personal fit' between you and the client. A good personal fit can salvage an otherwise mediocre engagement and the combination of a good personal fit and a good commercial fit is a strong indicator of likely success.

Your skills and experience

A conventional approach to marketing and selling would typically start with the client and indeed we have already selected the type of client that would be a good fit. In this case, however, it is equally necessary to focus on yourself. If you already know what kind of coaching you wish to offer (executive, business, life, financial etc) that is a great start. Many coaches make that decision for the wrong reasons. They may start by describing themselves as an executive coach, for example, because they believe (rightly) that executive coaches typically command high fee rates. However, if as an executive coach you have no experience as an executive it is likely to prove hard to convince potential clients that they should hire you to help them in that role.

By contrast, if your focus is on relationship coaching, anyone who has issues with their relationships may be willing to hire you regardless of their role in business or position at work. The key in that case will be your experience in both difficult and good relationships and, to a degree, your qualifications as a relationship coach or in dealing with issues in that field.

In deciding what type of clients you want to work with it is helpful to be able to link your preference in terms of a field of work as a coach (if you have one) and with an inventory of your own skills and, more importantly, your experience. If you have no immediate preference for a field of work as a coach, one way to decide is to start from your experience and skills base and build from there.

In my own case, when I began to coach, I had spent over 10 years reorganizing two large investment management businesses as their operations director and had held board level appointments for a number of years before that. I was interested in the reasons for the successes and the failures we had experienced in those reorganization projects and felt that I could add value for senior executives as a coach in helping them to overcome similar challenges.

In addition, I had a dozen years of Army service including two years at the British Royal Military Academy at Sandhurst. I therefore felt that I knew something about leadership and had honed those basic leadership skills over the rest of my career. I believed that I could therefore credibly coach business owners and managers around leadership issues also. By contrast, a recent MBA graduate told me that, because he had an MBA and the course included a leadership module, he felt able credibly to offer leadership coaching to senior executives, most of whom were many years older and more experienced than he was.

Apparently, he found it hard to get hired in that role.

In selecting the type of client with whom you want to work, therefore, your training as a coach is likely to be less relevant to the client than your real-world experience in both the workplace and life generally. Rightly or wrongly, my experience indicates that clients prefer to work with a coach who they believe has working experience in their field or of their current problems and ideally who has also coached in similar fields. This is borne out in a recent survey undertaken by ICF, which indicated that 'relevant experience' was an important factor in the selection of a coach for over half of all clients.

Your own journey to date, your experience and your learning all therefore become relevant both as indicators of what sort of clients you could credibly seek to work with and (perhaps more importantly) those with whom you could not or should not, at least initially. If a particular field of work interests you there is no reason to avoid it completely because you lack direct experience or expertise. Expertise can be learned. Experience is harder to achieve but not impossible.

In deciding how best to define your perfect client, you may find a table such as Table 2.1 helpful:

TABLE 2.1   Defining your perfect client

Factor	Explanation/considerations
Gender	This is relevant in cases where you wish to focus on clients such as women seeking promotion to senior roles or transitioning into them, or working mothers who find difficulty balancing the demands of job, family etc.
Age	I find that coaches often experience a degree of difficulty in coaching those who are significantly older than they are. The reverse is less often the case, although it depends on the issues around which the client seeks coaching.
Type of personality	You may prefer to avoid clients that have aggressive or abrasive traits, for example. You may also find it less easy to work with clients that have a particular psychometric profile. That is not to say that you should not work with them; simply that it is worth making a positive decision one way or the other rather than being passive.
Relationship status	If your chosen coaching focus is on relationship issues, this will obviously be a factor in client selection. Clearly, personal relationships will also have an impact, positive or negative, on other aspects of the client's life and work. Even if this is not the chosen focus of your coaching it may be relevant in client selection.

TABLE 2.1 *continued*

Factor	Explanation/considerations
Nature of the client's business or industry	This is obviously of greater relevance in the case of business or executive coaching. If you accept that relevant experience is indeed a factor for clients in their decision to hire a coach, it will help to target clients in an industry or profession in which you have some experience; preferably experience that is fairly current. Alternatively, there may be industries in which you prefer not to be involved due to your own personal convictions.
The client's role within their business	This is not quite as simple as the client's job title, although that may be a useful proxy. In my experience the use of a specific job title can be too limiting; I therefore favour a broader description such as 'senior executive'. You may also want to look at the type of function that the client will be in; for example operations or administrative roles as opposed to what in the banking or investment management world would be called 'front office' staff. In many firms operations and admin staff are under-coached and under-developed in anything other than pure technical matters, in my experience.
Size of the client's organization	A simple measure of size would be number of employees or (for a public company) market capitalization. That may be insufficient and fail to capture issues such as subsidiary companies that operate on an almost stand-alone basis. I prefer to think of this in terms of the firm itself or the division/department within which the client works or which represents their sphere of influence. I have worked with clients in very large firms where the individual client holds a senior position but their organization is in fact quite small. I also work with the owners of businesses that employ only a dozen or so people but have turnover measured in millions of dollars. This is very much a 'player's choice' issue and one which you may decide is not relevant for you.

TABLE 2.1   *continued*

Factor	Explanation/considerations
Common issues/ challenges in this type of role/industry	This factor focuses on the possible 'commercial fit' opportunities for you to work with the client. If you can identify areas where it is likely that the client may have issues and you can see how you might enable the resolution of those issues, you have a strong reason to approach the client and a good basis from which to articulate benefits and results that you can deliver. The issues may be at the industry level (eg law firms in the UK face pressure to consolidate) or at the individual level (senior partners find it hard to handle cultural clashes within merged firms)
Likely personal challenges or dreams for this type of client	This is a variation on the previous item but focused on the issues and desires of the individual: the working mother who wants to have both success at work, a happy and fulfilled family life and time to spend on art and music for example.
Values and behaviours	We have looked at this in some detail earlier in this chapter. In my experience, where a coaching relationship goes wrong or is less successful than either the client or coach would wish, it is most often due to dissonance in values and behaviours. To be willing to say 'No' and to decide not to take on an engagement is not only liberating but necessary on occasion.

What benefits do you uniquely deliver?

Clients will hire you because they believe that you are able to deliver specific results for them and that those results will be beneficial for them personally (as well as for their organization, family etc). We look at the ways in which you can articulate those benefits clearly and in language that resonates with the individual client in Chapter 5. However, there is a difference between the benefits that you deliver through your coaching and the benefits that can be delivered by coaching in general. We touched on some of the latter in Chapter 1. The benefits that you deliver will be specific to you and will form a key element in your personal branding or unique selling proposition (USP), which will also become the answer to the first killer question ('What do you do?').

The term USP was coined by a gentleman called Rosser Reeves (who rose to become chairman of advertising agency Ted Bates & Co) and was discussed in his 1961 book *Reality in Advertising* (published in New York by Alfred A Knopf). He stated that:

1 Each advertisement must make a proposition to the consumer. Not just words, not just product puffery, not just show-window advertising. Each advertisement must say to each reader: 'Buy this product, and you will get this specific benefit.'

2 The proposition must be one that the competition either cannot, or does not, offer. It must be unique – either a uniqueness of the brand or a claim not otherwise made in that particular field of advertising.

3 The proposition must be so strong that it can move the mass millions, ie pull over new customers to your product...!

Having considered your perfect client, you will have a fair idea of the kind of problems that such individuals are likely to experience and the degree to which you can credibly offer to enable them to resolve those problems: hence the need to take into account your own past experience, qualifications and skills set.

This combination of factors begins to outline the likely areas of what I call 'commercial fit' with your potential clients; in other words the areas where you can make maximum positive impact for them. That positive impact encompasses all of the benefits that you will deliver, but should be broken down to as granular a level as practicable so that you can better link your USP to the needs of your perfect client. The result will be to enable you to focus your business development and referral generation efforts.

For example, in a business coaching context, 'improving bottom line results' is a fairly good generic headline, but it might encompass several factors such as:

- improve the client acquisition rate for sales people;
- improve customer retention and referral rates;
- improve the profitability of each customer by increasing the number of transactions each makes and/or the profitability of each transaction.

Each of these is in fact a separate commercial fit opportunity and may represent a separate engagement for you.

Linking your USP to the perfect client

The benefits you seek to deliver have no meaning when taken in isolation. They must be benefits that serve your client by either overcoming a problem or fulfilling a dream or, if possible, both. They must also be relevant to the client at the moment when you are in contact with them. The reason is that clients will only buy when they are ready to buy and they will buy only when they feel a specific need/desire. It is very helpful if the solution that you offer to address that need or to fulfil that desire is broadly similar to the solution that the client already has in their mind (and in my experience clients will typically have some form of solution in mind when they meet you – or even when they search for someone like you on the web). To reiterate, however, the client is looking for solutions to problems or fulfilment of dreams, not usually for coaching as such.

Having looked in the abstract at the factors that define your perfect client (and indeed those that indicate what a perfect client is not), you can begin to encapsulate your USP/benefit ideas in a short statement in the form:

I work with XXX [type of client] who struggles with ABC [problem] or wants to XYZ [dream to be achieved] more effectively.

Later, you can add to that statement a short description of how you help these clients and then a third statement of the benefits and results they experience. As an example of an introductory statement where the perfect client is a senior executive in a corporation or the owner of a business, you might say something along the lines of:

A: I work with business owners and senior executives who find it hard to translate their strategic vision into real-world actions that their people understand and believe they can carry out.

Alternatively, if my perfect client was a time-pressed working mother, I might say:

B: I work with working mothers who struggle to balance the demands of family life, running a home and a job.

Ideally an individual who might be a good or even a perfect client for you will hear or read a statement along these lines and think 'That sounds like me...' or 'I recognize that problem...'. If they are able to do so, there is a good likelihood that they will start to ask questions and hence begin a conversation with you. If they are searching online for a solution to a felt problem, and your description resonates with them, they will make contact with you. We look in some detail at becoming as 'constructively visible' as possible, especially on the internet, in Chapter 3.

The next part of your description statement will be an outline of what you do for the clients who face the issue you have described, in a manner that once again encourages a conversation. The combination of the two will also serve to 'qualify' the person to whom you are talking or who is looking at your website; they will self-select and decide either to learn more or to move on. A client of mine refers to this as 'Buy or bye-bye' in his own business.

For example, in the case of my example 'A' above, the second half of the statement might be along the lines of:

I enable them to bridge the gap between their strategic business aims and their operational delivery capability.

In example 'B', it might be something like:

> I enable them to focus on the items that are really important to them rather than the noise of the demands on their time that simply appear urgent.

Note, however, that you do not necessarily have to describe in any detail how you do this, or even the general process – coaching, mentoring etc. You may decide to use the word 'coach' rather than 'enable' if that is the specific role that you wish to have with that client.

With that in mind, we can now add a final element to the statement that headlines the results that the client will experience. Ideally this should be in terms that the client can visualize, ie literally see in their mind's eye. This is because a significant majority of human kind has a visual learning preference (in other words they prefer to receive information visually). That does not simply mean that they like to see pictures, charts etc. It also includes the use of visual language and images; 'how will this look for you...', 'let's take a helicopter view of this issue'.

In my example 'A', I might say something like:

> The result will be to reduce friction in their business, by using the capabilities of the whole firm to best effect and avoid making promises to customers that they cannot keep.

In example 'B', it might be:

> The result is that they feel less stress and a greater sense of control because they can give themselves permission to drop, defer or delegate things that are less important for them.

Positioning yourself as an expert

We shall look at this from the point of view of becoming as highly visible as possible to potential clients – or rather to the type of clients that you want to work with – in Chapter 3.

However, at this point, it is worth noting that your business development efforts will be streamlined and become far more effective if you are recognized as an expert at some level: in other words you are seen as the 'go to' person in your field.

In part, this becomes self-generating as you work successfully with more and more clients. However, it will be important to ask every one of those clients for feedback on their experiences and, if possible, for positive testimonials that can be quoted on your website and elsewhere. This will help to reinforce positive perceptions of the kind of results you deliver and the way in which clients experience you.

There are some situations where this is not possible. For example, many of my own clients hold very senior positions in major firms. Most of them prefer not to acknowledge that they have hired someone like me to help them. In some cases it may be seen within their firm as a sign of weakness. In others it could be misinterpreted by stock-market analysts. I therefore undertake that I will never use their name or the name of their firm in any kind of marketing nor will I use them as references for other potential clients. That in itself can be seen as a powerful endorsement, even if it is non-specific.

Alongside your testimonial library, you can ask for 'recommendations' on sites such as LinkedIn (again, we look at the use of LinkedIn and other social media sites later in this book). You can link to those recommendations from your own website or quote from them as well as providing a link.

In addition, you can generate a sense of expertise through writing and speaking. By 'writing' I do not necessarily mean writing a book (although that can be highly effective). A 'tips' booklet is relatively easy to prepare and cheap to produce in hard copy (almost zero cost if done as a downloadable e-book). I produced two tips booklets at the request of clients; one called *105 Tips for Doing Well in Tough Times* and the other *101 Tips: Leadership Can Be Learned*. Either could have been used as a slightly costly but highly effective business card. They were formatted to fit in a typical business envelope and could be posted with a covering note for the cost of a normal letter. The content could also have been licensed for re-use in other ways and in other media. Had I agreed to a licensing deal, I would have insisted that my copyright statement still appeared as the author and that my contact details were also shown prominently.

Writing can extend to posting sound comments on issues raised in online forums that are relevant to your potential clients. If you do this, you will need to be quite active in a given forum in order to gain visibility. Most forums prohibit purely commercial posts. However, they will not usually ban the inclusion of the URL for your website in your signature block.

Lastly, writing can (and in my view should) include the preparation of what I call 'marketing collateral'. By this I mean articles (that may or may not have been published but are of a standard that could be published) on topics that are relevant to your audience of 'perfect clients'. In addition, you can prepare white papers, reports, focus notes etc on those topics. The report format is not the same as an article, in that it will usually be a 'how to…' or 'how to avoid…' topic, whereas the article may simply be a thought piece or commentary. We look at this in more detail in the next chapter.

The benefit of having a small library of such pieces is that you can offer to send a copy to a prospective client that you meet socially for example. Alternatively, you can offer a report, free of charge, in exchange for the name and e-mail address of a visitor to your website. By asking for the report, that person is giving an indication that they might be a potential client. However, it is unlikely that they will 'bite' immediately, so you will need to consider how best to maintain contact with them until they take a next step, whether that is to opt out of further contact from you or to buy from you. With that in mind it will be helpful to offer a range of services with different pricing levels so that a new client can take a baby step with you first at relatively low cost and hence lower perceived risk. Again, we explore service design later in this book.

In the next chapter we look at how to extend your professional network so that, having identified the 'perfect' client for you, you are able to connect with more of them.

CHAPTER SUMMARY

- Coaching is arguably something you do or an approach that you use to help a client, rather than something you 'are'. Other approaches including mentoring and consultancy may be more appropriate at times. Coaches willing and able to deploy these will usually be more versatile and hence better able to win work.

- The combination of the 'personal fit' with the client (congruence of values and behaviours) and the 'commercial fit' (the opportunity you have identified to make a significant difference for the client and/or the client firm if that is relevant) defines both the opportunity to do business and the likely success of the engagement.

- Defining the personal fit is about understanding the combination of both those negative factors that would rule out a client for you and those positive factors that indicate a likely positive relationship.

- Your credibility with a good potential client will depend on the role that you seek with the client and will be influenced by the client's perceptions of your past experience and expertise.

- The client must be able to visualize the benefits you deliver and those benefits must be immediately relevant to the client in question if they are to hire you. This begins with the answer to the first killer question, 'What do you do?' It includes a description of your preferred client, an outline of a problem such a client is likely to face and an outline of how you might resolve that problem.

- The use of 'marketing collateral' in the form of written articles, reports, tips booklets, a book, audio interviews, videos hosted on sites such as YouTube etc, helps to evidence your expertise. That can help to reinforce your position in the mind of the client and make it easier for them to decide to hire you, so long as other factors such as basic 'like and trust' are in place.

Marketing collateral

03

It is a myth that people buy coaching: they buy problem resolution or dream fulfilment. As mentioned in the previous chapter, coaching can be one of the approaches to achieving those results. In order to maximize the likelihood that a given client will (a) opt for coaching and (b) decide to hire you to provide it, you will need to raise awareness in their mind of both coaching as a highly effective approach to personal development and of the benefits you deliver. This requires a combination of education of potential clients and being visible to them. Your marketing collateral is the bedrock of both.

For any new connection that you make it will usually require several further contacts before that person is likely to be willing to do business with you. You can maximize both the number and the value of such contacts through the use of good, relevant collateral material. This can also help you to qualify potential clients further; in other words to filter out those where the commercial and/or personal fit is lacking in some way so that you minimize wasted time and effort in pursuing engagements that will not be fully effective.

In this context your marketing collateral means any item that can serve to increase awareness of you and the benefits you deliver as well as reinforcing your position as an expert in your particular field. These items can include:

- your website;
- any written material, such as flyers, reports, white papers as outlined below;

- material delivered at speaking engagements;
- video presentations;
- taster sessions and consultations (which may or may not be delivered free of charge).

There will be overlaps between these items so you will almost certainly be able to re-purpose ideas and material that have been used in one format for others. It will also be necessary to ensure that there is consistency of message between the various media you decide to use; it will obviously be counterproductive to express one set of ideas on your website and the reverse in a video.

The quality of each piece of collateral must be consistently high so that it reinforces positive perceptions of you and what you do. The subtle message you want the potential client to take away is: 'This person is a real professional. Based on what I see here, wouldn't it be good to get to know this person?' Not only must the quality of what you produce be high, it must also be relevant to the potential client, otherwise they will simply skate over it and may be less willing to give time to the next piece you send over.

Let's look first at your website.

Your website

A website is no longer a 'nice-to-have' item; it is essential, not just for coaches but for any business in my view. Indeed your website lies at the core of all your marketing activities. In most cases you will seek to drive people to visit the website ('traffic') not only in order to raise awareness of you and what you do but also to develop a list of those who could be good potential clients.

Once at your site, those people need to be able to find out, very rapidly, why they should remain (which they will do only if they find a specific benefit to themselves). Ideally the site will help the visitor to 'qualify' themselves (in other words to decide if the site is directed at people like them). If they are indeed part of the target audience for that site (in this case one of your 'perfect clients') they should be encouraged to register their interest by leaving their name and e-mail address in return for receiving something of high perceived value (something from your set of marketing collateral). In other words there should be a clear 'call to action' to visitors for whom the site is relevant.

Even if you make a personal connection at a conference or some other group event, there is a strong probability that the first thing that person will do before they meet you again is to look at your website. They will then probably search for you using Google or another search engine and will lastly look at your profile on LinkedIn followed by Twitter and perhaps Facebook. If any of these elements is missing or there is inconsistency between them, it will send an alarm signal. At the very least you will have a question to answer during that next meeting. Your online collateral therefore needs to be thought through as an integrated whole rather than piecemeal. We look at social media such as LinkedIn in more detail in the next chapter.

Even as recently as the early years of this century, it was not terribly easy for non-technicians to create a website and get it up on the web. By the same token, having a website built and hosted was not cheap. Today this is no longer the case. Anyone who is minimally computer literate can learn, very quickly, how to create a perfectly satisfactory website. If you prefer not to follow a DIY approach, you will find a host of technical people who will do the work for you for very little money.

A good source of such people is (anecdotally) Elance (**www.elance.com**). As you will see if you visit that website, Elance offers the opportunity to post the details of a job. People capable of doing that job can bid for the work. You can look at reviews submitted by previous employers and select the individual you wish to use. It is worth looking for language capability as a selection criterion as well as technical ability because you will need to be able to communicate detailed change requirements etc. Several similar sites exist, including People Per Hour (**www.peopleperhour.com**) and oDesk (**www.odesk.com**). Each has a some-what different focus and operating procedure so make sure that you understand what you are getting and the way in which you interact with the service providers before you go firm.

It is of course critical to ensure that the details of your job are accurate at the start. If you do not provide a clear and sufficiently detailed description of what you need the developer to produce, it is unlikely that you will get what you want at the price you agreed. In most cases, developers will undertake reasonable changes or tweaks to a site, such as correcting typos etc, free of charge, but anything beyond that will usually trigger additional charges. If you gain a reputation in that online community for incomplete project descriptions or for changing your mind, you may find it hard to get bids from the better developers; this is a two-way process, after all. I therefore highly re-commend that you write any content for your website yourself or alternatively hire someone to do it for you and ensure that you are happy with that content before you move on to building a site and importing the content.

In terms of time taken to get a job such as website design and build-ing delivered, the preparation of a detailed specification may well take as long as doing the work yourself. The choice to hire a devel-oper is not therefore usually one based on time saving (in this case) but on your technical capability and the willingness (or otherwise) to go through a learning curve that would allow you to follow a DIY approach. In my view, the level of technical skill needed to build a satisfactory website is now low enough and the benefits of being able to add or change the content of your site at will are so great that it makes sense to learn the basic skills necessary and go for DIY.

Your domain name

The domain name is also known as the URL (uniform resource locator) and is what someone will type into a web browser such as Internet Explorer or Google Chrome in order to access your website.

The choice of your domain name can have a significant impact on the ability of people to recall it and indeed of search engines to find your site and place it high in the ranking of search results based on the search terms entered by the user.

In most cases the domain name will simply be the name of your business preceded by www. and followed by something like .com or .co.uk. In setting up your business, not only should you make sure that the relevant limited company/LLC name is available (assuming you decide to operate as a limited company/LLC rather than as a sole trader) but that the relevant domain name is also available. It may make sense to buy the domain name before you register the company; there are individuals who look for newly registered businesses, then check to see if the relevant domain name has been registered. If not, they will immediately register it in several variations. The next thing you know will be a letter or e-mail offering to sell you those domain names at inflated prices.

In choosing your domain name, try to:

- Keep it fairly short.
- Avoid the use of hyphens and underscores (these make it harder for individuals to remember and also for search engines to index the site). If you use hyphens etc, you risk the possibility that potential visitors will type in the domain name without hyphens and find themselves at a completely different site...
- Where practicable use a key word in the domain name (such as 'coaching') – which is likely to be typed into search engines by people looking for the sort of services you offer.
- Where practicable use your business name as the domain name – it will make it easier for potential users to remember.
- If possible buy the domain name in several different forms including both the local format for your country (eg .co.uk, .de, .fr) and the international format (usually .com). I am sceptical about the use of formats such as .org or .net in this context.

To check the availability of domain names and to buy those you wish to use, simply look at the website of any major web hosting provider such as 1&1, Fasthosts, etc, or a specialist domain name provider such as UK Reg or GoDaddy. In most cases you will find a field into which you can type the name you wish to use. This will throw up a list of the available formats (.com, .co.uk etc). You can select those you wish to buy or look for alternatives. The typical cost to register a domain name is currently approximately £3 per year for a .co.uk name and £6 per year for a .com name. When you buy a domain name, I recommend that you set the renewal options to 'automatic' in order to avoid the possible loss of what might become a key business asset in the event that you forget to renew in good time.

Web hosting

In order to link your domain name and a website to the web, you will need to arrange hosting of that domain in a location where it can be accessed over the internet. In theory you can host your site on any computer that is connected to the internet. However, in practice, you will wish to buy hosting from a specialist provider. In most cases you will want to use a provider based in your own country. There are several reasons for this. For example, telephone support issues might be affected by time differences (if you are located in London and your hosting support is based in Los Angeles with an eight-hour time difference in 'normal' business hours...). If you are UK-based and your website is hosted in the United States, all website traffic including e-mail may become subject to the US Patriot Act, which (essentially) means that it can be open to inspection by certain US government agencies. Many UK government departments and certain other organizations require that all data relating to them is carried on servers based within the EU.

Web hosting is relatively inexpensive; a typical basic package will cost between £3 and £5 per month. That will allow you to host only one website, so if you plan to build several sites you may want to look at either what is called a 'reseller' package or to use a service such as that offered by HostGator in the United States where you can host unlimited sub-domains (effectively unlimited websites) for a single payment of around $10 per month. I used Fasthosts in the United Kingdom for a number of years but decided to switch to Heart Internet when I decided to host several sites via their reseller package.

You should ideally consider web hosting before you move on to building the website because the nature of the service you choose can affect the way in which you go about the development. For example, if you decide to use WordPress® (which is now the default choice of many professional developers as well as ordinary business and personal users) you will need to check that your hosting provider can accommodate a WordPress installation – the majority can; indeed most web hosting services now offer what is known as a 'one click installation' of WordPress onto a domain.

Building your website

If you decide to follow a DIY approach and develop your own site, three approaches that could work are:

- use a template based approach provided by your chosen web-hosting company;

- use a package such as WordPress originally designed for blogging and content management; or

- use something like 90SecondWebsiteBuilder, which is a WYSIWYG ('what you see is what you get') design program that automates much of the site development process and offers both a template approach and the ability to start with a blank sheet of paper.

The templates provided by a web hosting company such as 1&1 will do a perfectly good job of getting an adequate website up quickly and fairly painlessly. The linkage between buying your domain name, buying your hosting service and building your website can be almost seamless. It is a sound way for non-technical people to make a start. However, in my view, these services offer limited flexibility and there is a danger that you will end up with a generic site that does not say quite what you want about your business. The template approach is far better than nothing but it would not be my first choice.

WordPress (**www.wordpress.com**), is a piece of open-source software that was created as a way to enable non-technicians to put a blog online. The basic WordPress framework itself is free of charge. However, many of the add-ons available are chargeable – even though not usually expensive. It has been developed into a sophisticated content management system that allows anyone to build a website, add a blog (or not) and change or add content at will.

The learning curve involved in WordPress is quite small and I believe that most novices could learn all that they need in a morning by following some of the many online tutorials available. (Try searching online for 'free WordPress tutorial' and you will bring up over 20 million results). If you are willing to pay for professional online tutorials, you might take a look at those on offer from **www.lynda.com**.

A key benefit of WordPress is its inherent flexibility and the fact that you can use numerous add-ons (called either widgets or plug-ins) to add functionality such as secure e-mail contact forms, payment processing facilities, etc. There is a vast array of WordPress 'themes' available, which can provide a different 'look and feel' for a site at the click of a mouse or can enable a site to respond automatically to display optimally on the device on which it happens to be viewed (eg laptop versus smartphone). One point to have in mind, however, is that WordPress is constantly being updated. You will need to keep abreast of these updates in order to maintain the in-built security features designed to prevent the intrusion of malware, viruses etc.

An alternative, XSite Pro™ (**www.xsitepro.com**), was designed to enable online marketing specialists to design and build feature-rich websites quickly. It is a good piece of software and I have used it for a number of years to develop and update several sites. It automates much of the routine work of content management and in particular the process of changing the look and feel of pages across the site: a single change can be made to replicate across the whole site with ease.

XSite Pro is now several years old. The underlying structure of the sites it produces is a set of tables, which is not the most up-to-date approach. However, it works well and XSite Pro offers a huge variety of templates as well as the option to start with a blank sheet and re-tain complete flexibility of design. There is a learning curve in getting to grips with XSite Pro but the package comes with a comprehensive manual and online help functions.

I have recently started to use 90SecondWebsiteBuilder (**www. 90secondwebsitebuilder.com**), which has also been around for some years. It offers somewhat greater flexibility than XSite Pro and I think it is likely to become my weapon of choice for website construction.

A downloadable white paper on website design and building, includ-ing details of how to buy a domain name and find suitable hosting etc can be found at **www.successasacoach.com**. This also covers the basics of website creation software, the use of content management and blogging software such as WordPress etc.

Designing your website

In terms of the actual design of your site, some key points are as follows:

- Before you begin the design and build process, map out the main elements (how many pages you want, whether there may need to be sub-pages, the outline content and the purpose of each page etc) of the site and create a 'wire frame' or a diagram of the site on paper.

- Decide the general 'look and feel' of the site including how the pages will appear and in particular where the site navigation buttons will show up. There are two common placements for the navigation buttons: towards the top of each page immediately beneath any header graphic or in a left-hand margin. It is vital that the navigation is clear and uncluttered. Poorly structured and non-intuitive navigation is one of the greatest causes of visitors moving away from a site.

- The site should focus not on you and what you do but the type of people you seek to work with, issues that they typically experience and the results you deliver in enabling them to resolve those issues. Once again, it is a matter of focusing on the approach to answering the first killer question ('What do you do?') outlined above. This will of course need to be consistent across all of your marketing collateral and in what you say to potential clients when you talk to them.

- Each page on the site needs to have a headline that grabs the attention of the reader followed by a sub-head that gives them a good reason to carry on reading. In other words there must be a visible benefit to the person who represents your preferred client. You want those people to remain on your website as long as possible. If they are not your preferred clients, that should be clear to them and there is no harm in those people navigating away from your site. In other words, the design and content of the site should help visitors to pre-qualify themselves.

- Your site should encourage each visitor that is in your target audience to provide you with their contact details so that you can begin to develop a relationship with them over time. In other words, the basic 'like and trust' that can occur in a matter of moments in a face-to-face meeting will need to be built over time when the contact is online in written form. Visitors who request information from you can receive a periodic 'drip feed' of relevant items from your marketing collateral that allows them to 'get to know you' through your writing, video tips, etc (see below).

- That acquisition of contact details is done by way of a contact form linked to the offer of some part of your marketing collateral.

- It might be a report outlining the benefits of coaching (there is a redistributable version of exactly that available at **www.successasacoach.com**). It might be a tips booklet or something else that you have written which is of relevance to your audience.

- By completing a form that requires the name of the individual and their e-mail address and hitting the 'Submit' button (or whatever words you decide to use instead of 'submit'), the visitor can automatically be sent the material they have requested in the form of either an e-mail attachment or (more commonly) an e-mail containing a link to a separate web page from which they can download the relevant file. This process may sound unduly complex. However, it is required in order not to fall foul of regulations that control the use of e-mail marketing, such as the 'CAN-SPAM Act' in the United States and similar legislation in the United Kingdom that prohibits the sending of unsolicited commercial e-mail.

- The software that drives this process is called an 'autoresponder' and there are several of these available at a relatively low cost; some are even free of charge for a limited number of users or volume of e-mails. We explore this in more detail in the section on broadcast e-mails on page 96.

Content: keeping it simple

Your website need be no more than an online brochure with a simple structure involving a handful of pages. It must however:

- tell the visitor immediately who are your preferred clients;

- indicate the benefits to those clients of working with you;

- offer an opportunity to provide contact details (in return for downloadable material that is perceived to be interesting and relevant by your target audience);

- offer an opportunity to contact you by e-mail, phone and mail (I suggest that you use a contact form with a 'Captcha' (one of those automatically generated sequences of distorted letters and numbers that must be typed into a box on the form before it can be submitted) rather than a basic 'mailto:' e-mail address in order to minimize automatically generated spam coming to your inbox);

- if possible provide a few testimonials (these could be linked from your LinkedIn profile), plus any 'trust badges' such as certification by an organization like ICF or Worldwide Association of Business Coaches (WABC), membership of organizations such as the Institute of Directors (IoD) or a Chamber of Commerce etc;

- provide the same level of disclosure of items such as registered office for a limited company that would be required on a letterhead.

In terms of the basic page structure and content for each page, I suggest something along the following lines:

- Home page: gives your answer to the first killer question: 'What do you do?' based on the formula described in Chapter 2. You will need a headline that grabs the attention of the reader within three seconds, otherwise there is a high risk that they will navigate away from your site.

- An 'About' page: gives the visitor to your site an idea of who you are, your values and behaviours and your 'back story' – the journey that brought you to coaching and has informed your work. This should also reinforce the type of clients with whom you prefer to work.

- A page about how you help clients: this can be a series of mini case studies and/or a series of testimonials. The latter are of particular value if you are able to quote the name of the individual involved and their profession/name of their firm if it is relevant.

- A resources page: this is optional but can be a good way to offer more of your collateral material in exchange for a name and e-mail address.

- A contact page: this is essential and should show all available means to contact you. I use a contact form on my site in order to avoid my e-mail address being harvested automatically by 'spam-bots'.

I recommend that you show a good photograph of yourself (head and shoulders) on the 'About' page. If you have videos on YouTube, show links to these on the Resources page. As mentioned above, clear navigation is critical. I would provide links to the main pages immediately beneath the header graphic and a complete set of links including any sub-pages on the left hand margin column. I would also add a right hand margin column with an offer of a free report etc in return for the visitor's name and e-mail address. That offer should appear on each page in the site.

Adding a blog

It may be beneficial to have a blog linked to your website, but only if you can be certain to post regularly to it. To have a blog with a handful of posts, the most recent of which is several months old and where there are no comments, is counterproductive. In any event you will need to be able to add content to your website, be it in the form of blog posts or new pages.

In my view, the website is such a key part of your marketing and sales effort that it is worth taking the time to learn the basics of how to build and maintain the site yourself (ie to use a content management system). If you use a suitable platform such as WordPress for your site, that can be easy to achieve.

Keep the design 'look and feel' of your website as simple as you can. Follow the same rules of thumb on the use of colour, different typefaces etc, as we explore for your business card in Chapter 4 and you will not go far wrong. Although it is less of an issue than it used to be, have in mind that not all typefaces display accurately in all web browsers. Three typefaces are pretty much guaranteed to display as intended: Arial, Times Roman and Courier New.

Other marketing collateral

I think of marketing collateral not just as 'stuff you can give away' but as material that:

- reinforces your perceived expertise;
- provides relevant and actionable information to the recipient;
- has a high perceived value (and may have a high price tag shown, even if it is given free of charge);
- has a long shelf-life;
- carries your contact details.

That material will usually be provided in written form, at least initially. However, the ideas may also form the basis of a seminar or workshop session, a training package, a video tutorial that can be delivered online by streaming video or even YouTube as well as by DVD, etc. We look at each of these later in this chapter.

Some of these items can become products in their own right. A significant benefit is to offer what can be low cost (and hence low perceived risk) purchases for new potential clients so that they do not have to join a coaching programme in order to gain some insight into you, your approach, your values and behaviours etc. In other words, they are able to 'meet' you in a video and decide if they want to meet you in person. In giving away a product that has a price tag attached you are automatically implying a cash value to the gift and making it less likely that it will be ignored. A book that may be self-published but looks like any other trade paperback and has a £25 cover price is far less likely to be binned than 'freebies' that are offered as such.

Another benefit to you of having such products for sale is that it provides an additional stream of income and one that can be largely automated in terms of payment processing and delivery. The products you offer should be tiered in price, with a good range of items available free of charge. The first 'paid for' item might be priced at say £25, the next at £80–£100 and the next at say the £500 mark. We look at pricing further in Chapter 7 when we consider fee setting. Clearly you do not want to set prices for collateral material that cannibalize your fees for coaching.

Let's look at some of the various types of collateral you might need or want to produce.

Written material

Your business card

The most basic piece of collateral is of course your business card. We look at key points of business card design in the next chapter. It is worth taking a little time at this stage to think through the design not only of your business cards but of any written material you might produce so that it is consistent. Ideally the same design features should also appear on your website so that your material can become immediately recognizable by clients and potential clients.

A focus note

This is typically a one to two page document that gives specific 'how to...' information on a tactical topic such as preparation for meetings, which you know to be relevant to your potential clients.

A white paper

This is typically a four to eight page document on a more strategic topic such as good practice in running meetings; often entitled something like *Seven Errors That Make Meetings a Waste of Time – and How to Avoid Them*. The title will usually encapsulate a problem that is relevant to the potential client group and the sub-title will either expand on that issue or (more effective, in my view) offer a resolution.

A tips booklet

This can be an exceptionally effective vehicle for providing excellent, actionable information that evidences your expertise and can start the process of positioning you as an expert in a given field. You can of course produce several different booklets on different topics, each with a slightly different audience.

A tips booklet is also quite easy to write because each tip need be no more than a couple of sentences and there is no absolute need to link tips together as one would do in a full-length book. Each tip should be action oriented and specific. There is no set number of tips to include in a booklet; however there may be an expectation that it will be greater than 50 and probably less than 120. It seems to be a hangover from 1950s advertising techniques to use a title such as '101 Tips to ABC...'

However, when compiling the booklet, remember that the printed interior page count will be in multiples of four with the cover usually produced separately and representing four sides. Both MS Word and Office Libre offer templates for producing booklets so that you can submit print-ready material to a printer.

Tips booklets can be given away (usually in downloadable form) or sold either in hard copy or as a download. If you plan to produce a booklet in hard copy, set it up in a size that can be inserted into a normal business envelope (DL size in the United Kingdom) with a covering letter. Use good quality paper for the interior pages (I suggest 100 gsm or more) but not necessarily a card cover. The pages should be stapled through the fold in the middle of the book (known as 'saddle stitched' in the printing trade).

Make sure that your full contact details including e-mail, postal address and phone number appear both on the back cover and on the inside front cover, plus the company number, VAT number etc if relevant. Don't forget a copyright statement. This need be no more than the © symbol followed by your name (or the name of your business or both), the year in which the booklet was written and a phrase such as 'All rights reserved'. The benefit is to provide (theoretical) legal protection against the copying of your work. However, as I understand it, it is not possible to copyright ideas; what is protected is the way in which you express those ideas.

I recommend that you obtain an ISBN number for each booklet you produce and a bar code that reflects that number. The benefit is to allow your booklet to be sold on Amazon and elsewhere and this offers yet another mechanism for you to be found online. In the United Kingdom, ISBNs are assigned by A C Nielsen: **www.isbn. nielsenbook.co.uk**. You might also consider offering a licence to 'white label' your booklet – ie licence an organization to reproduce the booklet for a royalty fee. If you wish to do this, it should be stated on the cover, probably inside the back cover.

The cost to produce a tips booklet in hard copy is relatively small – typically less than £1 per copy even for a small run. That may sound like a fair amount of money but think of it as a more memorable business card that can generate leads and income in its own right. An acquaintance of mine, Paulette Ensign, based in San Diego, California, has made herself the go-to expert on tips booklets over many years. Find out more at **www.tipsbooklets.com**.

A full report

This will usually be in the form of a ring binder containing upwards of 80 pages giving detailed information on a given topic plus additional resources that can be downloaded or may be provided on a CD or DVD accompanying the report. A report will normally be sold rather than given away and the price will need to cover postage costs. The marginal cost to add a video once you have produced it is minimal; essentially the cost of the blank DVD and a slip case. The report has become seen as a somewhat old-fashioned format in which to provide information. However it can still be viable and the fact that it is now relatively uncommon may enhance its perceived worth. Once again, an ISBN, a bar code on the cover and a cover price that reflects the value you wish the client to perceive are at least helpful and arguably mandatory.

A book

This is the ultimate vehicle for positioning you as an expert in your field. It can be self-published or published in the traditional manner by a publishing house. If you choose the self-publishing route, it is essential that the finished article appears professional and looks like something produced by a 'real' publisher. The benefit of self-publishing is that you control the timeframe for production as well as the look and feel of the finished product. If you are fortunate enough to find a publisher, the time between completing a manuscript and the book appearing on the shelves can be up to six months. A book can be used as a somewhat costly business card to be given selectively to good potential clients.

In each case it is therefore essential that the item carries your name and contact details plus a copyright notice as outlined above. With a book, it is essential in my view, that it carries an ISBN number and bar code plus a cover price that reflects what it would cost in a book-shop. However, I recommend that you do not look on producing a book as a money-making opportunity. If you self-publish it will take time to sell enough copies to cover production costs. If your book is taken on by a publisher, royalties are a small percentage of the cover price.

If you plan to self-publish a book, it is vital that it looks at least as good as one produced by a traditional publishing house. The normal format for a 'business' book is known variously as 'trade paperback' or (in printers' terminology) as the 'modern European Royal format' in the United Kingdom and Europe. In the United States and Canada book formats differ somewhat. Rather than relying on arcane descriptions it is far better to decide on a specific size of finished page – eg 234 mm x 156 mm – to avoid scope for misunderstanding. Choose a size that matches similar books in your own location (standard sizes differ between the United States and the United Kingdom for example).

If you are self-publishing, I recommend that you engage the services of a good designer and of an editor with some knowledge of your subject matter. You may also want to engage a proof-reader (unless you are confident of your own abilities in this area).

There are a number of reputable 'print-on-demand' services that use digital printing technology to deliver short runs of books and in some cases a delivery capability. I've even self-published one title that was printed initially as a short run of 300 copies and I was very happy both with the process and the end product. For the author who wants to pursue the self-published route, even retail organizations such as Amazon offer a number of options to meet production, development and fulfilment criteria to ensure your work is available on their site. A quick search on Google will bring up a selection of print-on-demand suppliers and self-publishing companies.

As an alternative to producing your book in hard copy, you can of course produce for Kindle or another e-reader format. Details of how to go about this are beyond the scope of this book but you can find basic information on Kindle publishing at Amazon.com or .co.uk. Kindle is rapidly following in the steps of YouTube as a search medium for individuals looking for 'how to' information, although the vast majority of sales for the Kindle format are for fiction titles.

The ultimate confirmation of your status as an expert is of course to be asked to write a book for publication by a proper publishing firm. There are some issues to be considered before allowing euphoria to take over when you receive such an offer. For example, you will only receive a small share of the cover price for each copy sold, by comparison with a self-published book or a Kindle book. However, what you lose in the share of royalties, you will regain many-fold in terms of the marketing capacity of a professional publisher. You will also benefit from their infrastructure of editors, proof-readers etc, and their expertise on issues such as design, cover creation etc. There is also undoubted credibility in having your work published professionally by a firm that is recognized in the field.

The use of video

Video can be a two-edged sword. It can speed up the process of the potential client 'getting to know you' to the extent that they are keen to have a meeting during which you can explore the needs (or 'commercial fit') and decide if there is a real opportunity for you to make a huge difference to the client. If you offer coaching remotely (ie by way of a video-conference, Skype or telephone) a video is a good way for a client to experience what it may be like to work with you but also to see you in a way that is almost face to face. The client is able to do this in a manner that is entirely risk-free to them as they are simply observing you in action and have no need to interact with you. By the same token, video will work for you positively only to the extent that it is a medium with which you feel comfortable and where you can simply 'be yourself'. We explore the importance of this in Chapter 5.

YouTube or similar video

At its simplest, a video can be shot with a basic camera such as the Kodak ZE1 or Sony Bloggie, which can be uploaded to sites such as YouTube or Vimeo. You can host videos on your own website but that requires more technical know-how and (usually) an upgrade in the hosting package you use due to increased bandwidth usage. You also lose the searchability of YouTube and the ability of viewers to forward links to your video so easily.

The key to your ability to produce a satisfactory video is not really the technology, but to be comfortable that you can deliver an effective 'talking head' piece directly to camera, with minimal stuttering etc on a specific topic. It may not be necessary (or even desirable) to prepare a formal script if you know the topic well. The length of such a video need be no more than two to three minutes and should not be longer than five minutes. However, it must focus on a specific issue and how it can be resolved. This type of short video clip is a fine way for potential clients both to find you online (YouTube is the second most widely used search medium after Google) and to 'meet' you indirectly.

If you adopt this approach it is worth considering how to make a series of such videos and linking each to your website. Each video should ideally be edited to show the URL for your website and you could sign off at the end of the video with your name and the URL: 'I'm Joe Smith. Find more information like this at my website, **www.XYZ.com**.' You are of course looking to drive visitors to your website as outlined above.

A DVD tutorial

This type of video will normally be sold – or will at least carry a price tag that will enhance its perceived value if you decide to give away a copy. Again you can produce a series of DVD tutorials with elements able to be excerpted for YouTube. If you plan to produce full-length videos, you will need to invest in some more professional equipment, not least suitable lighting and an external microphone for your video camera plus some editing software such as Sony Movie Studio or Adobe Premiere Elements. There is also a significant learning curve to producing good quality videos. Alternatively you can hire a professional video camera operator who can offer a turn-key service. This is costly and may not always deliver the result you want.

Post-production issues such as producing a professional looking case insert, printing the title onto the DVD itself etc are not trivial but are essential if the finished DVD is to be seen as a good reflection of you and what you do. This type of video will almost certainly need to be scripted and will be shot as a series of linked sections each lasting three to five minutes. This is viable and helpful only if you feel comfortable in front of a camera. Video can be hugely effective if it appears professional and authentic. You will absolutely need to 'be yourself' on camera, something not given to all of us.

There is a downloadable report on 'guerrilla' video production at **www.successasacoach.com,** which contains more information on the necessary equipment, tools and techniques.

Speaking engagements

The ideas that form the basis of your tips booklets, reports, videos etc, can of course form the basis of excellent seminars or other speaking engagements. Not only does speaking in public enhance your visibility and offer significant networking opportunities, it is another excellent way in which to evidence your expertise. In a sense it matters little whether you are asked to speak on topics that are directly relevant to your coaching practice; you are a speaker, therefore you are by definition an expert of some kind. The fact that you have previously spoken on a topic other than your core expertise can in fact act as a great conversational hook later on.

For example, I was once asked to speak at a seminar held in Philadelphia on the subject of 'The Business Case for Sustainability' to an audience of mainly American lawyers and accountants, mainly from the Southern states. Perhaps predictably the atmosphere was somewhat cold as I came to the platform. However I was able to reassure them that sustainability did indeed have a solid bottom line benefit and was simply good business practice. The fact that I had made that presentation has been picked up by at least a dozen people to whom I have spoken subsequently at networking and other meetings and/or who have visited my website. Although by no means connected with my usual business activities, it has led indirectly to at least one significant engagement.

Many organizations require speakers. Clearly it is preferable to speak in front of audiences that are made up of your preferred clients. That may not always be practicable and it is often helpful to use speaking opportunities at other types of event to practise your delivery and simply become comfortable with the process of speaking. Opportunities may arise to speak at local Chambers of Commerce, Federation of Small Businesses (FSB) events, BNI or similar meetings, religious groups etc. If you are able to develop a number of presentations varying in length between 15 and 45 minutes, you can easily approach the leader of a chosen group and offer your services (usually free of charge) at a future event. If your topic is relevant to that group you will usually be welcomed.

Always ask the size of the group before you finalize your preparations; speaking to a group of a dozen or so is a very different experience from speaking to a group of a hundred or more. If there is any likelihood that you may need to have some sort of amplification (microphone and speakers etc) or a projector and screen for slides, I highly recommend that you check that everything is working before the event, or provide your own equipment. There is nothing worse than trying to use a PA system provided by a local hall that sounds distorted.

When you attend an event as a speaker, make sure that you have plenty of your marketing collateral available to give away at the end – certainly business cards and, if possible, tips booklets or reports that you are happy to hand out. If you've published a book, make sure you have supplies available for people to buy, or provide them with an easy way to buy it, for example through giving the link to its Amazon page. Where possible make sure that everyone present is strongly encouraged to visit your website, which is the engine room of your marketing and sales development efforts.

Taster sessions and consultations

Many coaches offer 'taster sessions' or consultancy exercises as a way to allow potential clients to experience how it might be to work together. In most cases these are quite short, say 30 minutes to 45 minutes and are delivered free of charge. I know of a number of coaches for whom 'free sessions' are the bedrock of their business development efforts. Whilst I accept that the potential client is likely to gain great value, even if the session is less than an hour in length, it is not clear to me that this is effective from the coach's point of view as a business-building tool. There is a danger that the coach focuses on 'selling' the free sessions and not on looking for paid work.

In my view, there is a place for free sessions as one part of the marketing and sales armoury of a coach, but only on a strictly limited basis. By that I mean that a free session might be worth doing if it is highly likely to lead to a significant paid engagement. That means that you might use a free session to convince a primary buyer (we look at the definition of primary buyers and several other roles in a client organization in Chapter 8) to hire you to work with a number of their people. You might use a free session with a gatekeeper to gain access to a primary buyer for similar reasons. However, given that time is your only finite asset and is non-recyclable, I recommend that you use free sessions sparingly.

Coaches who make significant income from their businesses usually offer services such as consulting and mentoring in addition to pure coaching engagements. A free consultancy or mentoring exercise can serve as a gateway to a larger engagement. However, once again these should be used sparingly in order to avoid the 'profitless prosperity' trap: lots of work but little income. I have developed a questionnaire that I ask any candidate for a free consultancy exercise to complete prior to a meeting and I make the meeting conditional on having a completed questionnaire in my hand three working days in advance. No questionnaire means no meeting. The questionnaire runs to four pages and, when completed, gives me valuable information that enables me to decide whether the client is indeed viable, whether there is a commercial fit and how best to focus the initial conversation so that I can deliver real value in the free session.

In my experience less than 10 per cent of those expressing interest in a free consultancy session complete the questionnaire. Those that do complete the questionnaire have a very high probability of following on from the free session to a full paid engagement. In other words, the presence of the questionnaire filters out a lot of time-wasters. A copy of that questionnaire is available from **www.successasacoach.com** in downloadable form. The website also offers the ability to download reports on the mechanics of producing each of the pieces of marketing collateral mentioned in this chapter.

Having identified who your perfect clients could be and considered where you might have a 'commercial fit' – ie an opportunity to deliver massive value to them – the next step is to work out how to locate and reach them. You will also need to think about how best to make an initial connection. This is far more than simple 'networking' in the traditional sense of going to networking groups and other similar meetings in the hope of coming across people with whom you get along. In the next chapter we therefore look at how to use the information you have developed so far to locate and become more highly visible to your chosen clients. In other words we shall look at the expansion of your professional network, both online and offline. Indeed the two are inextricably linked and it is a mistake to look at them as isolated activities.

CHAPTER SUMMARY

- Marketing collateral in its many forms allows you to evidence expertise (a form of social proof) and also enables the potential client to get to know you somewhat through reading, listening to or viewing your work. All of these approaches enhance your 'constructive visibility' to potential clients.

- Your website is the core of your marketing and sales activity. It is an essential item, not a 'nice to have' because it is the first place to which potential clients will turn in order to find out more about you following an initial contact. A well designed website that is search-engine friendly also maximizes the chance that potential clients will find you online.

- By using either the template designs available as options for most hosting packages or by using the default design provided within WordPress, it is possible to build your own website relatively easily.

- Follow known 'models of success' when designing your website (ie find other sites that work well and replicate the key design elements). Map out the layout on paper and write the copy for each page before you start to build.

- Look for opportunities to write articles for publication in trade press, guest posts on blogs read by your type of clients, tips booklets, a book, etc. Consider posting videos on YouTube showing you talking about issues that are relevant to your type of clients.

- Speaking engagements allow you to be seen and heard by people who may be potential clients. They can become a profitable side-line in their own right. Make sure that you have plenty of copies of some of your written collateral available as well as plenty of business cards.

- Your business card is one of the most important but least well-understood elements of your marketing collateral. It is important that it makes the kind of statements about you that you wish (heavy card, laminated finish, clear and professional typeface etc) and that what appears on the card encourages the person receiving it to ask questions and so begin a conversation.

- Some coaches offer 'taster sessions' free of charge. These can be a great way to enable the client to experience directly how it will be to work with you. However, it is important not to focus too much on 'selling the free session'. A coaching fishbowl can allow you to demonstrate your skills to a larger group.

Connecting with the right clients

04

Extending your professional network and winning referrals

In this chapter we are going to look at how you combine offline and online network building approaches in a way that focuses your efforts so that you minimize wasted time. It is important to integrate your offline network development and your online approaches (social media presence, website etc); the two are inextricably linked, although it is convenient to explore them separately here. We shall explore how to plan the development of your professional network and then implement the plan systematically. The benefit will be to avoid wasted effort and also to avoid 'forcing the fit' with individuals who are not in fact good potential clients.

'Forcing the fit' is a concept that comes from my hobby of woodworking. Having taken time to cut a joint, it can be tempting to knock it into place with a mallet or even the heel of your palm if the fit is not quite right. In many cases that causes one part of the joint to fracture. No matter how well it is repaired it will always look shoddy and will probably be more prone to break in the future, so it will usually be necessary to start again from scratch, with the consequent waste of time and costly materials. Much the same is true with potential clients that are not quite right for you.

Before we begin...

Before we begin, keep in mind that:

- People will buy when they are ready to buy and not before.

- Few people (even your near-perfect clients) will buy coaching as such: they will buy solutions to problems that they experience (which may include overcoming barriers to the fulfilment of a dream or desire).

- If they have a problem in mind they will usually have in mind a solution of some sort. That solution may be coaching or something that resembles coaching. However the client may not perceive it as such.

- If you sell (or are seen to 'push') coaching you may miss opportunities that could have been secured by thinking and talking in terms of problems to be resolved and results that you deliver. The process by which you resolve problems is not necessarily important in the mind of the client.

- You are looking to develop connections with people who fall into one of four categories (recognizing that they will move between categories over time):

  1 potential clients with a known immediate need;

  2 potential clients with a likely future need;

  3 people who can give you immediate referrals;

  4 people who may be able to give you referrals in the future.

Of these, categories 3 and 4 may prove to be of the greatest value to you over the medium to long term.

In developing your professional network, you are looking to make a reasonable number of high-quality connections, not necessarily to connect with every possible potential client in your field. By 'reasonable number' I mean enough that you can build a coaching practice that delivers your income needs and, over time, feel able to be increasingly selective in the work that you decide to undertake. By 'high quality' I mean people with whom you have a basic 'liking and trusting' relationship, who have the capability to give you business directly or to refer you to others who can do so and that match closely your definition of a perfect client – especially in terms of values and behaviours.

Constructive visibility

This chapter is essentially about building controlled and constructive visibility, being highly visible and positively perceived in the places that are frequented by the kind of people that represent good potential clients for you. The aim in each case is to make an initial personal connection that achieves a positive perception of you as an individual in the mind of the other person:

- allowing you to decide whether there is a 'commercial fit' (or if not, then a potential for referrals to people where there is a commercial fit) and failing either of these, whether you like the individual enough to keep the connection purely social;
- allowing you to capitalize on the initial connection by gaining consent to make further contact.

Your target audience: narrowing your field of play

Clearly, the more closely you have defined your perfect client, the easier it will be to locate people like that. The more specific you can be in defining your target market the easier it becomes to decide how best to reach people within it. Considerations will include:

- the nature of their work (not only for business or executive coaches but also in areas such as sports coaching and many other fields of coaching);
- geographic location (in particular if you plan to coach face to face, but this is likely to be a consideration in any event as

most clients will wish to meet you face to face before they start a programme with you);

- (for executive or business coaching) the level of seniority of the client and whether the client and the person who makes the buying decision are one and the same person.

For example, if my overall target market as a business coach were the legal profession, I might want to focus that down further by looking at:

- Fee earners in law firms (ie lawyers or para-legals) (because they will tend to be higher priority for coaching and other forms of development paid for by the firm). Although they will probably not be the decision takers in buying coaching, they will be involved in the selection of their own coach and can also act as a gatekeeper or introducer to a person who does take buying decisions.

- Partners in law firms (because they will be more likely to pay higher fees for coaching provided they recognize the value for themselves – or indeed to use coaching as a performance enhancement tool for their associates etc. They may be able to make a buying decision).

- Partners in law firms located in London (because it will be easier for me to visit them in their offices, ie there will almost certainly be a geographic consideration). Or even:

- Senior partners or managing partners in law firms based in London (because ultimately they control the budgets even though the HR or learning and development department may nominally have a budget...)

The narrower your definition of your target, the more focused your marketing efforts can be. The level of seniority you decide to target will reflect your view of where you can make a credible proposal to a client. This will, to a degree, depend on your own prior experience, qualifications etc (the 'personal journey' we touched on in Chapter 2). For example, if I want to work with lawyers, I could not credibly offer to coach partners around how to be a better lawyer, given that I have no legal qualifications. I could, however, credibly offer to coach them on business development and managing client relationships internally and externally. Having held board-level positions in large firms for many years, I can feel comfortable in working with partners in law firms and indeed senior or managing partners.

There may be a difference between the end client that you want to work with and the person you need to meet in order to gain agreement to work with their people or with their colleagues. That is an issue in the case of business or executive coaching and probably to a degree with sports coaching, but less so for life coaching where the buyer and the client are normally one and the same person. We look at the various different types of buyer and the role they play within an organization in the next chapter. For the time being, we just need to consider whether or not the person who takes the decision to hire you is the same as your perfect client. If they are different, you will probably need to be able to establish contact with both. That in turn may indicate two separate but linked approaches to building your network in your target market.

How and where to find good clients for you

Seeking out potential clients is not unlike looking for potential new friends. You will need to be present and constructively visible in places where the kind of people you would like to meet are likely to be found. In seeking to make yourself visible, you inevitably create the possibility of making a mis-step that damages otherwise positive perceptions of you. It may be caused by something as simple as asking a naïve question at a seminar, for example. This type of problem can be minimized by rigorous planning and preparation, without of course allowing yourself to become trapped in analysis. Nothing will happen in building your business if you do not take action.

Some coaches opt for a wholly offline approach to building their professional network; others prefer to work online. In today's world, one must combine the two in order to be most successful. In this context, I recommend the book *The FT Guide to Business Networking* by Heather Townsend (published by Pearson Education, 2011).

A giving agenda

A key mantra in building your professional network is 'give to gain'. When you meet a potential client where you can see a commercial fit, the question uppermost in your mind should not be 'How can I close this business?' but 'What can I give this person that is relevant to them and is linked to the commercial fit I have identified, in order to enhance our basic "like and trust" relationship?' We look at the 'like and trust' idea on page 104.

However, without that basic personal connection, I firmly believe that it will be impossible to win business and certainly not as a coach, because that relationship is inherently personal.

In terms of what you can give, think in terms of the various forms of marketing collateral we looked at in Chapter 3. One variation on the 'taster session' idea is to combine with a speaking engagement a taster session in the form of a 'coaching fishbowl' where an audience can observe you coaching a volunteer client. The benefit to the client of a fishbowl session is to gain good insights into an issue of their choice and to do so free of charge. You get to demonstrate, in the most practical way possible, your expertise as a coach. The audience can experience how your coaching could help them and gain a good idea of what it might be like to work with you. By contrast, a free taster session will benefit the client (and the coaching conversation might be deeper if the session is 1:1) but your expertise is not demonstrated to a wider audience as it is in a fishbowl.

Offline network development

If you need to be constructively present in locations where your potential clients can be found, the first issue is obviously to consider whereabouts (that you can reasonably access) will that be? In other words, where do these people gather and/or what media do they view, listen to or read where you can build a presence? Answers could include:

- at their place of work;

- at seminars/conferences/trade shows;

- at more specific networking meetings (for example BNI, FSB, The Executive Network (TEN) meetings);

- at meetings of a local Chamber of Commerce or similar organizations where networking is an adjunct;

- at meetings of other industry/professional groups;

- the relevant trade press;

- relevant/local radio/TV channels.

On the face of it, it might be hard to gain access to the place of work of potential clients. However, it can be done by, for example, offering to speak at an internal seminar on a topic that is relevant to the clients and points to a typical commercial fit for you with such an organization. Alternatively a coaching fishbowl might be of interest, but it may be better to look for a topic on which you can speak that resonates with that organization; a fishbowl could be a next step. In my case, I have spoken several times to groups of lawyers ranging in size from 6 to 30 on the topic of client acquisition and relationship development. In most cases, that has resulted in an engagement with the firm in question, although not always immediately.

Conferences, seminars and trade shows

It is rarely a problem to gain admission to these and in many cases attendance will be free of charge. Apart from the possibility of meeting good potential clients, another major benefit of attending is that you will gain a better insight into industry issues and questions that are hot topics for your clients. This in turn may well highlight additional commercial fit opportunities that you had not previously considered. Where you decide to go to a seminar, conference or trade show, it is essential to prepare beforehand, including setting your own expectations of what success would look like for you. A collection of business cards is usually worthless relative to one or two good conversations where you gain agreement to a follow-up meeting or even a phone call.

A preparation checklist and white paper can be downloaded at **www.successasacoach.com**. However, the key planning and preparation points are as follows:

- speakers and topics;
- guest list;
- questions you can ask;
- your answer to the question 'What do you do?';
- conversation starters;
- business cards;
- note pad and pen;
- dress code.

Knowing *who will be speaking* at a seminar or conference and the topics on which they will speak allows you to do some preparatory research and to think about interesting issues on which you can ask good questions. To ask good questions is a great way to be noticed constructively and is a legitimate starting point for conversations after the event. You may also find that one or more of the speakers is a potential client or someone who can refer you to potential clients, if you are able to make a connection with them.

The *guest list* will usually highlight a few individuals with whom you would like to connect. Knowing who will be present allows you to think about ways in which to open a conversation with them in a manner that is authentic and reinforces an initial positive perception. It is almost always better to make that *initial conversation* about the client than about you; most people prefer to talk rather than listen and most like to be asked about themselves and their experiences.

As for *questions you can ask*, once again preparation and some knowledge of the clients' industry will help enormously. Given that the aim is to be constructively present, good questions are a must. If you have no good questions, just keep quiet. The questions that others ask will usually offer good conversation openers later on.

The question *'What do you do?'* is the number one killer question. (The other two are 'What makes you different?' and 'Why should I hire you?'). What the client is really asking at this point is not about what you do or how you do it, but 'Why do I need to get to know you better? What's the benefit to me?' The answer 'I'm a coach' is therefore not enough. It may indeed be a 'box' that is better avoided because neither the term 'coaching' nor the benefits it can deliver are always well-understood and can mean different things to different people.

A better way to answer the 'What do you do?' question (as mentioned on page 45) is to combine a short description of your preferred client, with a statement of a problem that they typically face followed by the benefits you deliver in resolving that problem. For example: 'I work with partners in medium-sized law firms who find client acquisition hard. I help them to minimize the stress of marketing and selling so that they increase their hit-rate in meetings with potential clients. The result is that they improve revenue generation.'

The aim here is to pique the interest of the potential client because they recognize themselves in your description and hence feel encouraged to enter a conversation. If they are not one of those individuals you describe, or do not know personally someone like that, they will usually not seek to continue the conversation beyond the dictates of common courtesy. The result is that you save time by avoiding what would have been a wasted conversation from a purely business point of view.

The only way in which you can qualify and achieve a connection with potential clients is by having a conversation with them. In the vast majority of cases you will need to start that conversation. Having a few *generic conversation starters* helps to minimize your stress in approaching a stranger in a public space. That in turn will tend to increase the probability that you can make a decent initial impression and hence create the essential 'like and trust' that forms the base of a future relationship and allows you to explore the degree of fit for you with that person as a client.

The quickest way to get someone to talk is to ask a question. Possibilities could include:

- the number or type of people attending;
- what the other person had hoped to get out of the session;
- a point raised in the session and how it relates to the other person;
- how far they had to travel in order to attend.

Your business card

This is one of the most important pieces of your marketing collateral. We look at it in detail here rather than in the previous chapter because it is essential networking ammunition.

You should expect that people to whom you hand a business card will retain it, almost indefinitely, either in its original hard copy form or as a scanned image. (Many business people will use something like a CardScan® machine (**www.cardscan.com**) to avoid the need to enter data manually into their contact database.) Your card will say a great deal about you so it is important to ensure that the image it conveys is the one you want.

There is a short downloadable report on business card design and use at **www.successasacoach.com**. However, key points are as follows:

Size: a standard business card in Europe is 85mm × 55mm. In the United States it is 89mm × 51mm. Other countries have slight variations. Make sure that your cards are of the size commonly used in your country. Those who keep cards in a Rolodex or transparent folder are otherwise more likely to become frustrated that your card will not fit and bin it.

Thickness: a flimsy card conveys an impression of cheapness, which is almost certainly unhelpful for you. A reasonable minimum weight for a business card is 300 grams per square metre (gsm) with 350 gsm or more being a better choice.

Branded cards (which may be free of charge) showing the logo of the printer are to be avoided; they almost certainly convey an unhelpful impression.

Laminated finishes keep the card looking pristine for longer. If you decide not to print on the back of the card, leave that side un-laminated as it makes it easier for the recipient to write on (for example noting when and where they met you and any action points agreed).

Logos: if you use a logo it is essential to make sure that it looks professional and that it links to your business name or indicates the results you deliver for clients. Avoid using standard clip-art logos. (I have lost count of the cards I have seen carrying the standard pyramid logo used as a place-holder in MS Publisher). It can be worth having a logo designed professionally if you wish to use one. Otherwise, a typeface for the name of your business that differs from that used on the rest of the card will usually work. The use of colour for the logo may also help it to stand out.

Keep it simple: the client needs to be able to read two things immediately: your name and the name of your business if it is different. Other items such as your e-mail address, phone number, etc are essential but can come later. If you want to put a list of products or services on your card, consider using the reverse side.

Colour: avoid using 'reversed out' type (eg white on a black background): it is far harder to read. Have in mind that around 10 per cent of human kind has some kind of problem with colour perception, the most common being red/green colour blindness. The use of dark coloured type on a white or cream background avoids this problem.

Typeface: the typeface you use is a statement. If in doubt, stick with something non-controversial such as Calibri, Verdana, Arial or Times New Roman. To use something like Jokerman or even Edwardian Script may not be the kind of statement you want to make. Don't use too many different typefaces on your card.

Lastly, think of your business card as a conversation starter. Consider including as a 'strapline' below the name of your business – a phrase that encapsulates one of the results you seek to deliver for clients. My card includes the term 'Strategy Implementation' for example, which immediately begs the questions 'What does that mean?' or 'How do you do that?'.

Above all, make sure that you never run out of cards by carrying a backup supply.

As for your *notepad and pen,* if you are to follow up on actions you agree in an initial meeting with a potential client, you need to be able to record those actions and (often) the contact details of the person in question who may well not have come prepared with their own cards. A small 3-inch × 5-inch notebook or a few index cards of similar size will be invaluable. I have a leather note pad that has a pocket on one side for business cards and corner slots on the other to take 3 × 5 inch record cards.

Obviously you will need a pen or pencil to go with the pad. Once again, the type of pen you use will make a statement and people around you will take notice. A chewed Bic ballpoint will indicate something very different from a Mont Blanc (which of course you may feel is unduly opulent). It is helpful to use a pen that can be operated with one hand – eg pressing the top to push out the ballpoint nib rather than holding the barrel of the pen in one hand and rotating the top with the other...

In terms of *dress code,* conventional advice is to dress exactly as everyone around you. I prefer to dress one level up or if in doubt to go for a suit. In other words, if those around dress in chinos and open neck shirts, I will adopt a sports coat or blazer and also usually a tie. Perhaps the best way to sum up this item is in the words 'structured' and 'tailored'; you need to look the part – whatever that part may be.

I find it helpful to wear a jacket because it offers more pockets in which to carry essentials such as business cards, pad and pen, mobile phone etc. Ladies have the option of the handbag. However, if using a handbag, it is worth spending a bit of time organizing it so that business cards etc are readily found when required. I have recently bought a 'handbag organizer' each for my wife and for my step-daughter from Longchamp. This is a 'bag within a bag' that caters for phone, cash, credit-cards business cards etc. and can be transferred easily from one bag to another. It can be used as a small clutch bag in its own right.

Networking etiquette

The basic etiquette of networking is a combination of common sense and good manners. The approach you adopt in opening a conversation with strangers will be influenced by the type of event you are attending. If it is a straightforward networking group meeting such as a BNI breakfast, you will have a chance both before and after the formal part of the session to introduce yourself socially and get a sense of who is present and with whom you would like to spend more time. In the formal part of the session, you will have your '60 seconds of fame' when you get to outline what you do and the type of referrals that you seek. You can readily approach those with whom you wish to have a further conversation after the formal session is over.

This kind of meeting is a great way to gain confidence in breaking the ice with other business owners and allows you to hone the way in which you present yourself and your offerings. I have never found such meetings to be a huge source of business or of referrals. However, I know some coaches who built their entire business on the back of this type of meeting. The point is that every person attending a BNI or similar meeting is expecting to be approached by others present. In the aftermath of a professional seminar that may not be the case and a different approach is required.

As ever, planning and preparation helps to reduce stress and maximize success. If possible, you should identify before the event specific individuals with whom you want to speak. If you are able to secure an introduction from someone you know, so much the better. If not, search for the individual online in order to find a picture that allows you to identify them when you come across them. Do some research about them (again, the internet is a prolific source of data about far more people than you might expect) in order to develop a few specific conversation openers that you can plan and rehearse before the event.

When approaching someone who is already engaged in a conversation, look at the dynamic of the group to check that you can enter without causing friction. If only two people are talking and are standing close together (seemingly within each other's 'personal space') even though there is a reasonable amount of space around them, it may indicate that this is a personal conversation and it would be impolite to break in. This would be reinforced if they are leaning towards each other and have strong eye contact. If their spacing is more distant and their eye contact is less intense it is usually possible to approach from the side in a way that allows you to be picked up by their peripheral vision and be 'invited' to join in by one or the other moving back slightly. When the shoulders of the people you want to approach are 'open' – in other words the individuals are not facing each other directly – this can be seen as an indication that others can readily join their conversation. Shoulders that are 'closed' (especially if the individuals have their backs partially towards you) should be seen as an indication to avoid breaking in.

Rather than leaping straight into a pre-planned conversational opener, you might want to gain consent with a phrase such as 'I hope you don't mind me joining you...'. You can then continue with a question unless one of the group responds immediately. When you are engaged in a conversation, keep a reasonable degree of eye contact with the other person; it is social suicide to be seen to be looking over their shoulder for your next victim. Remember that your aim in engaging this person in conversation is to establish enough basic 'like and trust' that they will be interested in a further conversation that has a legitimate business reason and that is clearly relevant to them.

Don't outstay your welcome with any one individual. Make your desired connection; gain agreement if appropriate to a further conversation or to send them something from your 'collateral' library.

Anything more than about 10 minutes with one person is stretching things in this context. Make sure that you exchange contact details and then leave elegantly: explain that you have spotted an old friend on the other side of the room, or simply say that you want to leave the others to carry on their conversation. If nothing else comes to mind, excuse yourself to visit the bathroom or the bar.

On the last point, to have a glass in your hand makes it infinitely harder to manage things such as your note pad and pen or even retrieving a business card. It may prove wiser to take a drink at the end of the event if you want one or even to pick up an empty glass and leave it empty. It will give you a prop; something to hold onto and will also avoid possible spillage disasters.

Handing out your business cards can be tricky to accomplish elegantly if you are not asked for one. A good way to avoid a problem is to ask for a card from the other person. Once you have theirs it is perfectly reasonable to offer yours. When you receive a card, take a moment to read it. It is simple courtesy and you may pick up a nugget of information that kick-starts a different conversation. When putting away a card that has been handed to you, make sure that you put it in a different place than your own cards (and especially when dealing with someone of Asian origin, avoid placing it in the back pocket of your trousers; it is the cultural equivalent of using the card as toilet paper).

By wearing a jacket I know that my own cards can be brought out from my inside left pocket and cards I receive can go into my top outside pocket. Keeping the two separate avoids possible embarrassment. Before you pocket a card that has been given to you, ensure that you note on the back of the card (if you are not using your pad) the date of the meeting and any actions you agreed to take by way of follow-up.

Follow-up

Just do it! Rapid follow-up is an absolute requirement. Where possible send an e-mail to thank the individual for their time and confirm the actions you agreed. Sending a document by e-mail is fine but a hard copy sent by post with a handwritten covering note is exceptionally powerful; not least because relatively few people bother to do so. A hard copy document with a covering letter is far less likely to be intercepted by the 'secretary filter'. It may even be appropriate to send an e-mail explaining that you have sent a hard copy by post and to let you know if it does not arrive in a reasonable time.

Never Eat Alone...

This is the title of an excellent book about network building written by Keith Ferrazzi (published by Doubleday, a division of Random House, 2005). The title points to the kind of mind-set that those wishing to develop their professional network need to adopt. Other key points include:

- networking must be planned and methodical;
- building and maintaining your network requires time, so it must become a scheduled activity, in addition to using what might otherwise be 'dead' time such as a taxi ride between meetings;
- your network must be constantly nourished and reinvigorated or it will die quite rapidly (in other words you need to communicate regularly with those in your network with information that is relevant to them);
- you should expect to initiate communication most of the time;
- seek to give in order to gain (that includes making connections between members of your network for their benefit rather than yours).

A point that is less commonly mentioned is that there is a practical limit to the size of the network that you can maintain through personal contact (meetings, phone calls etc). There is no practical limit to the size of the network that you can support digitally. We look at the mechanics of how to do this later in this chapter.

The maximum number of personal contact relationships is usually assessed at approximately 150, based on research carried out by

British anthropologist Robin Dunbar. This figure is known as 'Dunbar's Number'. When your combined professional and personal network exceeds this number it may be necessary to decide who should be moved to a 'digital contact' relationship, because it is usually more effective to maintain a smaller number of closer relationships than to attempt to address a greater number of more shallow ones. The latter is a key feature of social networks that have redefined the meaning of the terms 'friend' and 'connection'. We explore this further in Chapter 10.

For a slightly different view of professional network building, you might want to take a look at the book *Network Your Way to Success* by John Timperley (published by Piatkus Books in 2002 and reprinted in 2004). Timperley is a former Partner at PriceWaterhouse, the major accountancy and professional services firm. His approach is as stereo-typically British in tone as that of Ferrazzi is American.

Online network building

Many of the same considerations apply to building your network in the online world as in the offline world. The mechanics will, of course, differ. However, as mentioned above, rather than thinking of these as two distinct activities, it will be essential to integrate them and to acknowledge that online has not replaced offline network development, simply changed it. The ready availability of highly qualified/targeted information is a huge benefit to you as well as to potential clients looking to find people like you – provided that you have taken adequate steps to create and manage your online presence. Where to start?

Your online network building strategy has three key elements:

1 your website (which, as already discussed, lies at the core of your marketing and network development activity);

2 your social media presence;

3 a broadcast e-mail capability.

We have already looked at the requirements for your website in Chapter 3, so will focus here on your social media presence and the use of broadcast e-mail.

Social media

There are now many social media sites available both for business and for personal use. Three of the best known on which we shall focus are:

- LinkedIn (**www.linkedin.com**);
- Twitter (**www.twitter.com**); and
- Facebook (**www.facebook.com**).

I recommend the book *Get Up To Speed With Online Marketing* by Jon Reed (Published by Pearson Education in 2011 under their FT Prentice Hall brand) if you wish to explore social media in more detail. Have in mind that the social media field changes rapidly and that you will need to allow time to keep your knowledge current.

LinkedIn has become the default social media site for professionals seeking to build their online profile and improve their professional network. In my view, it is essential to be present there even if you do not use its facilities fully. LinkedIn offers a basic service that is free of charge and a paid-for, premium service with many additional features. I believe that the free service is perfectly adequate for most purposes.

In order to make the most of LinkedIn, it is essential that your profile is complete and accurate. That will include having a good photograph of yourself (a basic head and shoulders portrait is all that is needed and you can/should use the same shot on your website), a couple of recommendations (testimonials) and all the elements of your biography including education and employment history complete. LinkedIn will flag missing elements and indicate the percentage of completion. You should also show the URL of your website. Once your profile is complete, LinkedIn will suggest possible connections based on your education and employment history. You can also import your own contacts database from MS Outlook and several other sources. This gives you the opportunity to establish connections via LinkedIn. Having in mind the 'Dunbar Number' mentioned above, I am sceptical of the value of having very large numbers of connections on LinkedIn. However, one must also appreciate that the relationship that one establishes via LinkedIn with people that you do not know personally is usually at a different level than that in a personal 'face to face' acquaintance let alone real friendship. That being the case it is possible to communicate via LinkedIn with a far broader but shallower network.

I am also somewhat sceptical about the potential to make good connections beyond people I have previously met (even if I have not seen them for a considerable time). However, I know people who have done so by explicitly seeking an introduction to a third party via an existing connection. They have identified that their contact is connected on LinkedIn to a third party to whom they wish to gain an introduction and have requested that introduction either directly or using LinkedIn. This is a variation of seeking a referral and we look at referrals specifically on page 98.

Twitter is a micro-blogging site that allows users to post short (140 characters maximum) messages to their followers. It is an excellent way to draw the attention of contacts to things such as new blog posts on your website. It is relatively easy to build up a significant number of followers on Twitter, especially if your posts are both cogent and amusing. However, it is far harder to ensure that these followers are relevant to you in terms of being good potential clients. In other words, whilst I am sure that Twitter has its uses for short broadcast messages, I have not found it to be a great source of either business or referrals.

Facebook, like Twitter, has had huge amounts of publicity and is one of the most visited websites on the planet. It is still largely used by younger people for purely social purposes although that is beginning to change and indeed Facebook is seeking actively to develop its 'business' audience through business related services and targeted marketing and advertising approaches intended to rival those of Google. It has also launched Facebook Business Pages.

I feel that it is as yet too early to tell whether Facebook can be used successfully by coaches to develop their professional networks. However, I am somewhat sceptical given that, for most people, Facebook is still seen as a social rather than as a business medium. In any event, it seems to me that the 'friends' one might glean on Facebook are unlikely to be targeted so one would likely waste considerable effort in sifting out reasonable business opportunities. I do not use Facebook myself, so I confess that these views are pure personal prejudice.

Whichever social media sites you decide to use, it is important that the data you put online is accurate and consistent, both between the various social media sites and also your own website, any CV you may hand out etc. It is also vitally important that you take time to manage your online profile and ensure so far as possible that adverse comments/material do not appear.

Use the privacy settings on sites such as Facebook for example with care. As a general rule, once any material is put online it can be in-credibly hard to remove it, so make sure that what you put up yourself is what you want others to see for a considerable period of time.

E-mail marketing and broadcast e-mails

We have looked above at how to collect names and e-mail addresses of visitors to your website who wish to download some of your marketing collateral. The use of e-mail can help to develop a relation-ship with those potential clients, which is an essential precursor to any decision to do business with you.

E-mail marketing has several advantages including very low cost to deliver and equally low cost to add new people onto your list pro-vided that the process is automated. It is however subject to some strict regulations that ban the sending of unsolicited commercial e-mail ('spam'). Although convictions are relatively rare so far, fines can be large. With that in mind, whilst it may be tempting to buy a list of names and e-mail addresses that appear to be good potential clients it is to be avoided. Even if they have given permission to be sent 'relevant offers' the permission has not normally been given to you but to the list provider. In reality, bought lists typically produce low response rates. It is therefore worth spending the time and effort to develop your own list.

You can speed that process by finding joint venture partners, ie someone who already has a relationship with people with whom you would like to do business but is in a different and non-competing market. They may be willing to promote you to their list of customers in return either for a share of the income you derive as a result or for a similar offer by you to your client of their services. That offer will of course need to be appropriate given your positioning with your clients.

In terms of how you send out large numbers of e-mails, it is perfectly possible to send each one manually from your own computer to people on your list. If your list is larger than a couple of dozen names, however, this rapidly becomes tedious. It may also put you in breach of the terms of service for your Internet Service Provider. I therefore suggest that you use a separate provider for both your autoresponder mechanism and e-mail marketing.

The autoresponder process of handling requests for material will normally be what is called 'double opt-in' where the person requesting a download from your site must confirm that request before they can access the material. Two of the better-known autoresponders are AWeber (**www.aweber.com**) and Constant Contact (**www.constant contact.com**). An alternative that offers a service free of charge for up to 2,000 subscribers is MailChimp (**www.mailchimp.com**). However, as I understand it, that free of charge service places adverts for MailChimp onto the e-mails sent out. That may not be an issue for you, but it is worth checking.

If you plan to follow up with further informational or promotional e-mails after the initial response, that should be made clear to the website visitor. They must also be given an option to 'unsubscribe' – ie to cease receiving e-mails from you. You should also have a privacy policy available to read. The safest privacy policy is to the effect that you will never make available the visitor's data to any third party unless required to do so by a court order. When you send an e-mail to your list or to a sub-set of it, make sure that there is a sound business reason for doing so. Nothing causes people to unsubscribe faster than receiving irrelevant e-mails.

Linking it all together

It is possible to link your activity on various social media sites, for example a LinkedIn update can trigger a Tweet to your followers automatically. The key is to think of your network development as a set of integrated activities and to plan them holistically. As for the mechanics of how to achieve this, Jon Reed's book is a good place to start.

Referrals

We have touched on referrals several times. It is sometimes easy to mistake referrals as of secondary importance in your business development activities. In my own case, however, the vast majority (I estimate well over 90 per cent) of my business over the last dozen years has come as a result of referrals.

If you arrive at the point of an initial meeting by way of a good referral, the complex process of building basic 'like and trust' is short-circuited and the cards are usually stacked in your favour. This is due to what I call 'transference'. For example, you know Fred. Fred understands what you do and the benefits you deliver. Fred is a friend of Alice and knows that she can benefit from working with you. If he is able to introduce you to Alice and at the same time to establish you in her mind as a possible solution of her problem, you gain by transference the credibility that Fred has with Alice. If she likes and trusts Fred, she will be pre-disposed to like and trust you also.

To win referrals is therefore at least as important as meeting potential clients directly and you should plan your network building programme accordingly, online and offline. With that in mind, to be able to define specifically your perfect clients enables you to describe in detail the kind of referrals that you would like to receive.

Don't confuse a referral with an introduction or a lead. A referral positions you in a role that you have chosen with a person who is a known potential client and who has an immediate need for your help. It also sets up a call to action, usually a suggested phone conversation to set up a face-to-face meeting if appropriate. An introduction is essentially social. It is better than nothing but it will take at least one further meeting to decide whether this person can be a client imminently, may become a client in the future, or may be no more than a possible generator of referrals. A lead is even more remote: simply a name and phone number or e-mail address and a suggestion that 'You mention my name when you call'.

It can be useful to help in the preparation of a referral. In one case, a client offered to introduce me to a banker (a good potential client for me at the time) who was a former Marine. His team was having difficulty winning larger deals and despite success with many small ones they were running way below budget. The eventual referral was along the lines of: 'Stephen is also ex-military. I know he can help your people to hunt the elephants you need with a .50 calibre Barrett rather than a .22RF. I have asked him to call your PA on Monday to set up a short meeting with you.'

In less than four dozen words the referral had:

- Established some common ground (the military connection).
- Highlighted the client's problem (hunting 'elephant' deals unsuccessfully).
- Positioned me as someone who could up-gun the team and did so in terms that were relevant to the individual (the Barrett .50 is a weapon of choice for Marine snipers. It fires the same round as the Browning heavy machine gun and is capable of dropping an elephant in its tracks at half a mile. By contrast

a .22RF is one step up from an air rifle and suitable to hunt rabbits at around 50 metres).

- Proposed an action (I should call his PA on Monday to arrange a meeting).

Good referrals are hard to come by but are gold dust when they do occur.

Having now arrived at the point where you are making connections with good potential clients for you, the next step is to explore how best to handle the all-important initial meeting.

CHAPTER SUMMARY

- People do not typically buy coaching as such – they buy problem resolution. However, they may have an image of coaching in their mind as one viable solution. Extending your professional network starts with building 'constructive visibility' among your target clients. It is essential to combine online and offline approaches.

- The narrower your definition of your 'perfect client' (your target market), the easier it is to focus your efforts.

- By following a 'giving agenda' (ie asking 'What can I give this person?' rather than 'How can they help me?') you tend to enhance your position in the eyes of potential clients and encourage each of them to give back to you. Your marketing collateral is vital in this context.

- In seeking to develop your network offline, consider where your perfect clients can be found, eg industry seminars and trade shows, and ensure that you are there also – and visible by way of asking good questions at seminars or speaking well at one.

- Prepare thoroughly before attending a seminar, conference or trade show. Know why you are going along, who you wish to meet and how you might best be able to do that. Have in mind some specific aims.

- Ensure that you can answer succinctly and credibly the first killer question: 'What do you do?'

- Ensure that your business card is well designed and that it is likely to encourage conversations – by what it says.

- Dress the part, whatever that may be. If in doubt, go for the suit option. Carry a pen or pencil that matches your look in order to take notes on the back of business cards you receive about actions you have agreed.

- Never forget the power of a handwritten follow-up note with a piece of your marketing collateral in hard copy; it is far more powerful than a two-line e-mail.

- Follow up rigorously and continue to do so with relevant material sent at reasonable intervals until the potential client either says 'Yes' or unsubscribes.

- Link your online network expansion to your offline efforts. Focus your activity around your website. Use the website to capture automatically the name and e-mail address of interested parties in return for sight of a report/white paper that is of relevance.

- Make good use of LinkedIn and Twitter. Add Facebook if you feel it is appropriate for your preferred clients.

- Use e-mail marketing carefully. Never buy in lists of prospects. Use the 'double opt-in' approach and a good auto-responder such as AWeber or Constant Contact. Seek referrals actively especially in the aftermath of being hired by a new client; that is the moment when they should be delighted with their decision. By all means ask again on the back of a successful engagement.

Meetings: how to plan and run them for success

So far we have looked at identifying the right kind of clients for you and on making an initial connection with those where you feel there is a good personal fit and also a sound commercial fit, ie you can see opportunities for you to make a major positive difference to that person by enabling them to resolve a problem or to fulfil a dream.

That initial connection may have come about by way of a referral (so much the better if that is the case) or some form of conversation in a public or semi-public situation. It may have started by way of a visit to your website that resulted in the leaving of a name and e-mail address, which you have followed up with a series of e-mails providing relevant content of good quality that has encouraged the potential client to take a positive action by contacting you. In whatever way it has occurred, that connection has been sufficiently positive that the potential client has agreed to a meeting with you.

Whether that initial 'formal' meeting is face to face or by telephone/ Skype matters little; a phone meeting is like any other except that technology intervenes. A phone meeting is of course harder for both parties because you lack the visual clues that form a significant part of the 'para-language' that conveys so much of the meaning we take from a conversation. That para-language includes facial expressions, gestures etc. However, you will still be able to listen for changes in tone of voice etc, which will become all the more important. In whatever form the meeting occurs, it will determine quite rapidly whether or not you wish to – or will be able to – win business from this person. The probability of success can be increased significantly by:

- the way you prepare the ground for the meeting;
- the way in which you conduct yourself; and
- the way in which you articulate the value that you will deliver to this person.

The first and second items relate to the perceptions that the potential client forms of you, which are vital and which we explore in more detail shortly. Note that I have focused on the person rather than the 'firm' or the 'organization' here. Even if you are an executive or business coach, where a firm may be paying for your services rather than the individual being coached, there is in this critical initial meeting no such thing as 'the firm' – only the person who is sitting across the table from you. It is that person who will decide whether or not to hire you, not 'the firm'. During this meeting several things must occur in order that you can move forward, which may mean a further meeting rather than a binary 'go/no go' decision to work together. You must:

- re-establish or reinforce basic 'like and trust', which must have occurred in your earliest contact with the client in order that you have reached this point (in other words, you will confirm the basic personal fit);
- confirm the commercial fit opportunity;
- find out what actually drives the client at a deep emotional level;
- decide how you can best help the client;
- articulate not simply how you can help but the specific benefits you will deliver and the consequent results that the client will experience; and
- identify the next logical step and 'ask for the business' (or at least for an agreement to move to the next step with a reasonable commitment to ensuring its success).

Many of these factors are in fact two-way: you and the client must both experience sufficient 'like and trust' to feel comfortable that you can work together; both of you must feel congruence of values and behaviours; both of you must see the commercial fit, etc.

Perceptions you generate

It is a truism that we have only one chance to make a first impression – good or bad. It is equally true that we are always creating perceptions whether we are trying to do so or not. The problem is that in my experience few people really understand the perceptions they generate, especially when they feel under stress (as you may when you go into an important initial meeting). As a result, they may make what are in themselves minor slips that generate in the mind of the client just enough of a negative view that they say 'No thanks'. This is akin to professional level athletics where the time difference between the gold medallist in an Olympic 100 metres event and the silver medal winner is measured in tiny fractions of a second. In business, there are no silver medals; the decision is binary – win or lose. The factors that separate win or loss are similarly tiny in themselves.

Initial perceptions are formed very rapidly – typically in seconds rather than minutes. This is a hangover from prehistoric times when 'fight or flight' decisions had to be made rapidly in order to ensure survival. Those perceptions may not be factually correct. However, once formed, they rapidly become reality to the client who will then tend to look for factors that reinforce their perceptions and to discount factors that challenge them.

In Gestalt terms, simple awareness is in itself curative. The fact that you are aware of generating perceptions in others and of adjusting your behaviours to enhance positive perceptions will tend to set you apart from others who lack such self-awareness. However, that self-awareness should not detract from a key element of success in your interactions with clients, which is very simply to be yourself, recognizing that you cannot be anyone else.

Meeting mind-set: being yourself

Many – indeed I believe most – people go into a 'formal' meeting with a sense that what is about to occur is in some way different from a normal conversation. They go through a ritual of mental preparation and place themselves into a frame of mind that is their 'meeting mode'. As a result they become more formal, less warm and friendly and less conversational. Essentially they are doing what an actor does before going on stage or onto a film set; they are moving into character and that character is necessarily different from their persona when they are simply 'being themselves'. Clearly, a consummate actor can convince the audience that they are in reality the character they portray. However, very few of us are good actors, let alone consummate ones.

By moving into meeting mode, we stop being ourselves. That causes considerable stress; it is hard to be someone other than yourself. More importantly, there is a very strong probability that the client will pick up on your stress and that it will cause dissonance. In extreme cases, it will bring about a reversal of the 'trust' element of 'like and trust'. By contrast, if you simply allow yourself to relax and just 'be yourself' the level of stress is reduced, you gain in self-confidence and hence you gain in terms of perceived sincerity and credibility with the client.

Rather than putting yourself into 'meeting mode' therefore, focus on simply being yourself when you go into any meeting and in particular that all-important initial meeting with a potential client.

There are of course variations on 'self'. What we are looking for is your most relaxed, in-control, professional self. We can observe this by way of a combination of body language and speech patterns. In my experience, the latter are more important and ultimately easier to control. You can telegraph physical relaxation by simple tactics such as sitting back in your chair and, perhaps, crossing your legs – although women may find this harder to achieve with elegance than men. If you avoid crossing your arms, you are signalling openness. Constant touching of your face tends to signal nervousness. Good levels of eye contact signal interest and engagement (although an unblinking, messianic stare is obviously to be avoided...).

As for speech patterns, the simplest and most effective idea to remember (but one of the hardest to follow) is of course to be conversational.

Gaze aversion in conversation

This is a term used by psychologists to describe the momentary act of 'looking away' or breaking eye contact when a person is digesting information. This is perfectly normal and occurs routinely during conversation. A great deal happens during these moments of gaze aversion. Essentially the break of eye contact allows a combination of reflection and visualization; the individual is thinking and building a picture in their mind's eye of the idea they are trying to digest. This process takes a fraction of a second to accomplish but is essential to the ability of the individual to comprehend what they have just heard.

More importantly, during that momentary gaze aversion, the individual is incapable of hearing additional information as the brain is fully occupied with the reflection and visualization process. It is akin to a computer 'buffering' as it downloads a video clip; during that process the combination of RAM and processor are unable to handle additional commands or more data.

Why is this important in the context of conversational speech? There are two key factors:

1 The natural pauses that occur in conversation allow the gaze aversion process to occur without interrupting the flow of ideas.

2 By the same token, if you 'talk over' the break in eye contact, the client is (literally) unable to hear what you say during that moment and hence eventually loses track of the logical flow of ideas so that they become unable to keep up with what is said and hence cannot arrive at your logical conclusion and take a decision, whether that is to agree or to disagree.

The result is that the client will be unable to say 'yes' (because they have been unable to take on board enough relevant information) or may have in their mind a picture that is radically different from what you intended. By looking for the momentary gaze aversion and pausing until eye contact is regained you avoid these problems. Similarly, it is hard for most people to listen and to write (eg take notes) at the same time. If the client is writing, it will pay to pause in order that they can complete their note taking before you add further information.

PowerPoint

There may be occasions when you feel a need to produce a PowerPoint deck to support a meeting with a client. Rather than 'talking through the deck' it is in my experience more effective to have the conversation as outlined in this chapter and use the deck as a 'leave-behind' that acts either as a reminder to the client of what has been said or that enables them to brief colleagues on your meeting.

Remember, however, that 'too much information confuses'. There has been a considerable amount of research into the amount of information that the human brain can handle in short-term memory. A hypothesis put forward in the 1950s that became accepted as fact is that most human beings can handle only seven data items (+/− two). (More recent research indicates that the number of random data items that can be handled simultaneously by most human beings is in fact lower, probably of the order of four to five.) However, if we accept the initial hypothesis, more than nine different items of data will overwhelm the ability of most people to understand and to follow a logical flow. With that in mind a PowerPoint deck that comprises more than nine slides will lead to confusion. The reason is the phenomenon known as 'recency' where people will tend to recall the facts that they heard most recently and will drop from their short-term memory facts heard earlier.

Conversation is the new PowerPoint

If you are simply being yourself in a meeting, it is easier to be conversational in your speech patterns; the two are inextricably linked. Conversation can be defined as random word groups, as opposed to sentences. We learn to read in sentences but during a conversation we do not talk like that. We produce a flow of ideas that may be connected in our minds – and which can be connected by the minds of our listeners. In part, the ability of the listener to make the connections is the result of the para-language mentioned previously.

If we were to type out verbatim a piece of recorded conversation, it would be very hard to read because, not only would it lack punctuation, it would lack conventional written structure. As an example of conversational speech in written form, you could look at sections of James Joyce's novel *Ulysses* or parts of his book *A Portrait of the Artist as a Young Man*. If read aloud, these make perfect sense: they are essentially conversational speech or a 'stream of consciousness'. However, they are hard to understand otherwise.

Critically, however, conversation delivers two significant benefits: it is by definition two-way and the use of conversation slows down your delivery (by comparison with a typical presentation mode). That allows the client to keep pace with your ideas and to interject comments, observations and questions, all of which help them to buy in to your ideas and indeed to feel that the conclusion is one that they have co-developed. What you say can therefore be more readily understood and acted upon. How does this work?

The use of conversational speech patterns creates natural pauses in your speech. If you are under stress (ie not really being yourself...) those pauses will tend to be shortened or you will tend to fill them with noise – 'err' and 'umm' sounds that act as fillers and give your brain time to formulate the next idea. We use these filler words because we are afraid to lose the thread of our own ideas by allowing the client to interrupt. In fact there is no thread because the ideas have not been thought through properly prior to the meeting. Either way, the uninterrupted flow overwhelms the capacity of the listener to keep up with what is being said. The naturally occurring pauses of conversation overcome this problem by encouraging questions and comments; the client is literally buying into your ideas by talking about them.

Conversation has been described as 'mutually agreed interruption' and the two-way interaction that helps to define conversation is essential to understanding of ideas as much as it is to developing and reinforcing a personal connection between the parties. The point is that through conversation you enhance your credibility with the client as well as learning vast amounts about that person and what drives them. By encouraging a two-way exchange, facilitating the asking of questions and the making of observations you help the client to cement in their own mind the value of your ideas. They are enabled to visualize the benefits you will deliver and can consequently say 'yes' more easily – if there is indeed a commercial fit.

Ensuring success in meetings

The fact that conversation is the new PowerPoint is an indication of why most meetings fail. Most meetings are run as monologues rather than dialogues, with ideas presented in linear form. Because of the failure to use a conversational approach, the capacity of the listener to understand is overwhelmed as outlined above. This is symptomatic of the fact that the typical meeting process runs counter to four key rules of communication:

1 Most people prefer to talk rather than to listen.

2 Too much information delivered verbally, without pauses for reflection, visualization and hence comprehension tends to confuse the listener. The result is that no decision will be made.

3 Experience indicates that the concentration span of most people is less than 15 minutes. In any event their decision in principle will usually have been made within this timeframe.

4 The purpose of communication is to gain a response rather than merely to pass on data.

With that in mind it is essential to set up the context of the meeting to ensure that it can be successful. This starts with making a plan.

Planning each meeting

General Eisenhower reportedly said that plans were in themselves useless because no plan survives contact with the enemy; however the process of planning is vital. In preparing for a meeting, your ability simply to be yourself and to manage the perceptions you generate will be enhanced and your stress levels reduced by making a plan that allows you to control the first few minutes of a meeting. Thereafter the meeting will take on a life of its own. The controlled beginning will, however, help you to feel in control by minimizing the number of variables at play. If you feel less stress and therefore relax, the client will tend to do the same, which further improves the likelihood of success in that meeting. If you are able to plan the meeting and control the early stages so that the client is encouraged to do most of the talking, you gain information on which to base your articulation of the value you deliver. You can therefore adjust your word choice so that it resonates with the client.

I highly recommend that you plan each meeting or phone conversation before the event. I use the planning tool below:

FIGURE 5.1 Meeting planner

Date	Time	Location or Dial-in details

Who will attend?

Who MUST be there?		What is their role in this meeting?	
Your firm	Client firm	Your firm	Client firm

Your Actual Aim in this meeting (Note: This may not be the same as the Stated Aim...):

Your Stated Aim in this meeting (the exact words that you will use to the client):

The Results you wish to achieve (in the words that you will use to the client):

Result 1	
Result 2	
Result 3	

The Questions you will ask to identify 'Fit' and what drives the client:

Question 1	
Question 2	
Question 3	

The time and location fields are simply a reminder for yourself. The list of those to be present and their roles in the meeting serves two purposes, especially if the meeting is a 'complex' one where more than you and the client are to be present. Firstly it can help you to minimize the numbers attending: the greater the number, the more complex the meeting and the harder it will be to succeed. The role of each person is especially relevant in the context of executive or business coaching where you are dealing with a complex organization. The 'role' here is not their job title or their position in their firm's hierarchy, but their role in relation to your engagement. We look at the various roles in this context in Chapter 9. However, in summary, some examples might be:

- primary buyer: the person who has the authority to hire you and 'write the cheque';

- gatekeeper: controls access to the primary buyer;

- technician: may be asked to 'sign off' that you have the necessary expertise and/or that the structure of the proposed engagement is sound;

- ally: someone within the client firm who is willing to act proactively as an advocate for you and your ideas;

- forward observer: someone within the client firm who is not in a position to act as an ally (or feels unable to do so) but will tell you 'where the political minefields are';

- end client: the person you seek to coach (who may also be the primary buyer).

Each of the individuals in the above roles will need to be handled separately and the nature of your relationship with each of them will differ.

The aim of the meeting is simply what you seek to achieve. This may not match the stated aim, especially in an initial meeting. The actual aim of any initial meeting is to achieve and to reinforce basic 'like and trust'. Clearly it would be counterproductive to state that explicitly to the client. Your stated aim will therefore be different; something like 'To talk about your business'. Your stated aim will need to be open and non-threatening; it is designed to help the client to talk after all. In a business or executive coaching context, most clients will be happy to talk about their business and indeed may be less happy to talk about themselves at this stage in your relationship. In a life coaching context, a better stated aim might be 'To talk about you'.

The results that you seek to achieve from this meeting should be quite specific. Whilst the stated aim is open, these results are highly focused and it is towards these that the meeting will be directed. In a business context, I might use something like:

- to understand the outcomes that drive your success at work and how you measure them;
- to learn what factors you feel are most likely to get in the way of achieving those outcomes; and
- to agree next steps.

In a life coaching context, the results statement might be something like:

- to understand where you would like to get to and over what time frame;
- to learn what feels like it is causing you friction in your journey there; and
- to talk about how I might enable you to overcome those friction factors.

In both cases these are highly results focused. The reaction of the client when they hear these desired results will help to indicate whether they are really ready to be coached or if they simply want to talk at this point with no clear idea of areas in which they want help or how they might be helped. The latter is in itself not a disaster; a key output from this initial meeting is to gather information about what is going on for the client and what drives them emotionally.

Lastly on the planning tool, we have questions that you can ask to identify the needs of the client. The questions you ask will of course direct the conversation and also the sort of information you can gather. You gather information by getting the client to talk and the quickest way to get someone to talk is of course by asking a question. We shall look at how best to ask questions later in this chapter.

When you are filling out the meeting planner, take time to word-smith each entry so that it is as effective as you can make it. The stated aim, the results statements and the questions need to be good enough for you to use, with comfort, in the meeting and in your pre-meeting communication. By getting them right on the planner, you can save considerable time on the pre-meeting communication and also reduce stress for you and for the client in the critical opening moments of the meeting itself.

Pre-meeting communication

Having spent some time planning the meeting, you can now begin to use the information on the planner. Your pre-meeting communication can achieve a number of positive outcomes. It:

- establishes you in a role that you prefer with the client;
- differentiates you from others in your field;
- positions you as someone who is results oriented (assuming that is what you want);
- focuses the conversation and so saves time; and
- allows the client time to think and so to prepare for your meeting in a way that helps to reduce their stress and so improve the likelihood of a positive outcome for both of you.

Don't forget that this is not an adversarial meeting. It is one where you seek to direct the conversation towards a goal that, if it is achieved satisfactorily, will be positive for both of you. The client agrees to hire a coach who can make a significant positive difference to them and you as that coach are enabled to carry out an enjoyable engagement where you can help a good client to achieve results they never thought possible and (all being well) gain excellent referrals on the back of it.

Before any initial meeting and indeed before most other meetings, I send the client an e-mail or hard copy letter that is timed to arrive three to five working days prior to the meeting. We shall explore which medium is preferable shortly. On the face of it, that communication is simply a confirmation of the logistics. It is in fact far more than that. A typical example, based on my role as an executive coach might be:

Dear Ms Client

I am looking forward to our meeting on [date] at [time] at your offices. My aim in our meeting is to talk about your business so that I can understand what outcomes you feel will drive your success and what factors are most likely to get in the way of achieving those outcomes. In that context I can outline some of the benefits I can deliver in overcoming those 'friction' factors and we can agree next steps.

In order to focus our conversation and save time, I would be grateful if you could please think about your answers to the following question before we meet:

What do you feel are the most important factors that drive your success and how do you measure them?

1

2

3

4

5

Other

I look forward to meeting you on [date]

Sincerely

If you look back at the examples we considered earlier, you can see that the pre-meeting letter/e-mail is taken almost verbatim from the completed planner. In other words, once the planner is finalized, it is a matter of (almost) copying and pasting the relevant content.

E-mail or letter? I often send both, with the e-mail acting as a cover note to the letter that is attached. There are obvious benefits of sending an e-mail with your pre-meeting communication. The client may not be in their office until the day of your meeting and so will not see a hard copy letter sent by post until it is rather too late to be of use. Many younger clients use e-mail as their preferred communication mechanism and see anything in hard copy as a hindrance or at best old-fashioned.

In short, there is no one 'right' answer; it is a matter of 'player's choice'. However, for clients aged over about 50 who were not brought up on the use of computers, there is some power of nostalgia if nothing else in sending a hard copy letter. However, the letter needs to be printed out on good quality paper – at least 100 gsm in weight and on a decent printer. Whether your printer uses ink-jet or laser technology is irrelevant as long as the output is clear and without smudges or over-runs. If your letterhead shows up on screen as being in colour, you should expect to use a colour printer so that what the client sees in hard copy matches what is seen on a computer screen. With some clients in Germany, where the fax machine is still used as a primary means of business communication, I will often fax a copy of the letter over.

Whether you send a letter by post or by fax, the receipt of hard copy will usually avoid the 'secretary filter', which might simply delete an e-mail unread. If I send a fax to a client, it is quite usual for the recipient to hand-write their answers to the question(s) I ask onto the letter and then fax it back to me. Otherwise it may be scanned and returned by e-mail. If I send an e-mail only, rather than both e-mail and letter, I often receive no response prior to the meeting. There are obvious benefits in having answers to your question(s) in advance as you have more opportunity to prepare.

At the start of the meeting

The purpose of the planner and the pre-meeting communication is to help you to control so far as possible the critical first minute or so of the meeting. If you have received answers to your question prior to the meeting, take a copy with you. Otherwise, take with you a copy of the pre-meeting e-mail or letter you sent.

Focus on simply being yourself and being as relaxed and conversational as you can; this is all about perceptions. Once any necessary introductions have been made and any water, coffee etc, has been poured, simply repeat, verbatim, your stated aim and the results you seek from the meeting, using exactly the same words as you used in your pre-meeting letter. The client has seen these same words before, so knows that there are no surprises – hence no potential threat – and can therefore relax and enjoy the rest of the meeting.

At this stage it is tempting to 'start the meeting' in earnest. In fact, I recommend that you never allow the meeting to start. Remember that this is not intended to be a formal meeting but a conversation. You can even use the phrase, 'Before we begin...' so that, in the mind of the client, the meeting is not yet in progress and they can therefore remain relaxed. Next, if you have received answers to your question(s) prior to the meeting, you can ask the client to talk through them. Otherwise you can ask if the client has received your letter and had time to think about their answers to your questions. If so, they can be asked to talk through them; otherwise you can hand over your copy of the letter and ask them to take a moment to read it and then answer your question. Remind the client that the benefit to them of this approach is to focus the conversation and save time.

In the vast majority of cases, the client will simply nod and say 'OK' when you reiterate your stated aim and the results you seek to achieve from the meeting. In doing so they have, psychologically, accepted your proposal and all that remains is to agree how your proposed aim and results should be achieved. By contrast, if the client is not minded to follow your proposal, they have an explicit opportunity to say so and to offer an alternative. In my experience, on the very rare occasions this occurs, the alternative offered by the client is quite similar to what I had proposed and is therefore easy to accept.

The statement of your aim and the results you seek at the start of the meeting essentially inverts the usual meeting process where the conclusion is the end point of a linear presentation that the client must follow step by step in order to be able to come to a decision. By stating the aim and results upfront, you create a psychological imperative to reach what has become a mutually agreed conclusion. This process alone also starts to differentiate you from others in your field.

By getting the client to talk through their answers to your question you can begin to gather information on multiple levels. It is therefore time to engage every ounce of active listening at your disposal. Where possible, I suggest that you avoid taking notes. The reason is that note taking can make it harder to hear at a deep level what the client is really saying – or perhaps not saying. I do not propose to enter the 'multi-tasking' debate here. However, I firmly believe that it is extremely hard to listen and take notes at the same time. Where appropriate, and with the consent of the client, you might consider bringing with you a colleague whose main job will be to take notes for you. Alternatively (again if appropriate and with the consent of the client) you might record the meeting using a small digital dictating machine. These can be bought for relatively little money – less than £50 – and can record several hours of conversation.

You are in fact making use of most of your coaching toolkit at this stage, listening, reflecting and challenging where necessary. In a sense this initial meeting is a highly structured and focused coaching session.

Gathering information

The purpose of asking questions and getting the client to talk is to enable you to gather information. This goes far beyond the basics of the commercial fit and typical business needs/opportunities. Of course you will want to check that these are still valid and learn more about them. Far more importantly, however, you need to understand what drives the client at an emotional level, which is where decisions are made – to be justified subsequently by logic. You can also look for clues about the way in which the client takes buying decisions and their learning preference. You may be able to make an informed guess as to the psychometric profile of the client but I feel that is best left to a later time as there is already a lot going on.

There is an old saying to the effect that a wise woman looks for reasons to back up her intuition. I believe that many men follow a similar approach but may find it harder to acknowledge that they possess intuition let alone use it. Human beings tend to make decisions emotionally, rather in the manner that they form perceptions about individuals or even animals that they encounter. They will then go through a process of (self-) justification. However, the decision is unlikely to be altered.

As a practical example, my main form of transport was for many years a motorcycle. It was practical as I could park free of charge in London (whereas a car would cost upwards of £25 per day to park in the same area). Fuel costs were lower than most cars as the bike delivered around 55–60 miles per gallon. I chose a machine called the Deauville, made by the Japanese manufacturer, Honda. It was a model used by many of the despatch riders in London at the time (as is its successor) on the grounds of bullet-proof reliability. After running that bike for some seven years and 75–80,000 miles I decided that a replacement was due. Logic said 'Buy another Deauville'. Emotion said 'The Deauville works well but it's boring. Those BMW 1200s that the police use look much more fun...' Three weeks of internal debate and the development of (superficially) logical arguments saw me order a BMW 1200 RT with all the trimmings at a cost that was over 50 per cent more than the new Deauville.

In listening to the client's answers to your questions you will be looking for information at four levels:

1 confirmation of the commercial fit;

2 the way the client takes buying decisions;

3 the client's learning preference; and

4 the psychological and personal drivers of the client.

The commercial fit is reasonably easy; it is either present or not. The degree of fit may differ from what you hoped but the fit should be clear. If it is not clear then you will no doubt find it hard to articulate the benefits you can deliver to the client. Remember that the commercial fit in this context is defined by your ability to make a significant and positive impact for the client and one that is immediately relevant to them.

The way in which the client takes buying decisions will be indicated by their choice of language. Whilst it is not quite as simple as the 2 × 2 matrix in Table 5.1 below might suggest, buyers tend to fall into one of four types (or sometimes a combination where one is predominant with a secondary preference). Their preference will be indicated by the nature of their interaction with you and the type of language they use.

TABLE 5.1   Types of buyer

Relationship focused: Relationship buyers will seek to get to know you personally before they agree to do business. One client of mine insisted that we spend an hour 'telling each other our stories' as he put it before asking, almost as an afterthought 'When shall we start?'	**Partnership focused:** These individuals are quite rare. They will ask about how the engagement can be a win for both parties.
Transactional: These people will tend to talk in terms of speed of delivery and price.	**Informational:** These individuals will seek to understand in detail the process of an engagement and will want to discuss how it will work, what will be the impact on their colleagues etc.

In each case we are looking for the language clues that indicate where the client sits. This can help you to adjust your approach accordingly.

The concept of learning preference will be familiar to most coaches; it is essentially a description of how the client prefers to receive information. There are various models but one that is relatively simple is that developed by Neil Fleming, known by the acronym VAK (or sometimes VARK). The acronym stands for:

- Visual;
- Auditory; and
- Kinaesthetic (sometimes called 'Tactile').

Once again we are looking for linguistic clues. Visual learners will tend to talk about how things look for them; use visual images such as a 'helicopter view' etc. They will usually find it easier to see information presented in graphic form; pictures, graphs etc. Auditory learners will ask how an idea sounds to you or will tell you what they have heard. They may not maintain eye contact whilst you are talking, even though they are clearly engaged in the conversation, because they are accessing what they hear and eye contact can act as a distraction. Kinaesthetics are quite rare. You will often see them shifting uncomfortably in their chair as they (literally) 'get comfortable' with your ideas, which may need to be repeated in a somewhat different manner several times before you see the visible relaxation of the client as they gain comfort. The majority (around 70 per cent) of human kind have a visual learning preference so if in doubt you should opt for a visual approach in describing the value of your ideas.

Next steps

Having used structured questions and a conversational approach to get the client to talk as rapidly as possible in your initial meeting and thus gained a considerable amount of information on several levels, the next issue is how to link what you have learned together with your expertise as a coach so that you can articulate to the client the value that you will deliver for them if they agree to work with you. Once the client understands the value and the benefits you deliver, they can make the linkage with the cost (your fee) more positively so that price becomes a secondary issue in their buying decision. We look at the concept of value in the eyes of the client in the next chapter.

CHAPTER SUMMARY

- There is no such thing as 'the firm' – only people; because it is a person who will take the decision to hire you, or not as the case may be. Success in winning business is therefore founded on establishing basic 'like and trust' as rapidly as possible in the early stages of the relationship.

- Like and trust is based on the perceptions you generate. These may or may not be factually accurate but they become reality to the person who holds them. That person will typically look for factors that reinforce their perceptions and discount factors that challenge them.

- Positive perceptions will tend to be formed more easily if you are simply 'being yourself' rather than attempting to adopt a different persona because you are 'in a meeting'. The dissonance caused by the stress of adopting that different 'meeting' persona is enough to damage like and trust and hence ensure that you do not win business. It is also far harder work for you!

- During conversations, you will see the other person break eye contact momentarily from time to time. That allows inward reflection and visualization of the ideas just expressed. During that gaze aversion, the other person literally cannot hear what you are saying and the linear thread of the ideas is lost. Natural conversational pauses minimize this issue.

- Too much information confuses so that no decision can be made. Research on the number of distinct ideas that the human brain can handle simultaneously has produced different answers over the course of several decades. The 'magic number' of 7 +/− 2 held sway for many years. However, more recent research indicates that the figure may in fact be about half that number.

- Meetings must be planned in order to maximize success. The meeting planner (downloadable from **www.successasacoach.com**) allows you to pre-craft the vital first 30–60 seconds of any meeting and helps to ensure that you do not stumble over your words.

- A pre-meeting e-mail or letter setting out the stated aim of the meeting, the results you seek and one or two questions to focus the conversation will both differentiate you from others in your field and ensure that the meeting gets off to a good start.

- At the beginning of the meeting, reiterate the aim and results. The client will usually nod and say 'OK'. The hard part of the meeting is now over as they have agreed to follow your verbal road-map. Your pre-prepared question(s) then serve to get the client to talk as rapidly as possible. During this initial information-gathering phase, you are looking to:

  - confirm the commercial fit and the personal fit;
  - ascertain what drives the client emotionally (ie at a personal/psychological level);
  - gain clues as to the way they take decisions and their learning preference.

  so that you can better articulate the value you will deliver to the client and why they should hire you.

Value in the eyes of the client

06

In this chapter we shall look at how to structure and then articulate your offering in language that resonates with the client and ensures that they can visualize the benefits they will experience. The benefit to you is that the client will find it easier to say 'yes' and price will tend to be minimized as a factor in the buying decision. The result is that engagements can become more profitable and hence you can (ultimately) become more selective in your choice of clients and the types of engagement you prefer to undertake. This is perhaps where rubber begins to meet road; if the client cannot (almost literally) see the value you deliver they will not be able to say 'yes'.

What does 'value' mean?

Value is on the face of it a very concrete concept and many people will interpret it in terms of 'positive bottom line impact' – in other words some form of financial benefit. In my experience, that is by no means how clients always think. They may have in mind something far softer (or rather, less easily measured) such as feeling empowered, feeling enabled to handle complex or conflicted relationships more easily etc. One of the factors not always considered in the ROI for coaching is simply the fact that the coachee feels better about themselves and their ability to handle difficult situations.

By going through the information gathering process outlined in the previous chapter, you gain an insight into how the client will assess the delivery of value to themselves through your coaching engagement. Indeed that process sets up a context in which you can easily ask specifically how the client will measure success if they were to hire you. It is invariably more effective to ask for specific information rather than to make assumptions, even if the assumption is well-informed. Once you form a view or learn specifically how the client defines success or prioritizes the benefits you can deliver, you can then begin to build in your own mind a basic value equation. Against the benefit you deliver you have to assess, from the client's standpoint, the cost to them of the mechanics of the engagement as well as the financial cost.

The basic value equation can therefore be seen as:

$$\text{Value} = \frac{\text{Benefit (as defined by the client)}}{\text{(Financial cost + 'Hassle')}}$$

Clearly the result of that equation will need to be positive (and ideally strongly positive) if the client is to say 'yes'. We look at this in more detail when we look at fee setting in Chapter 7. However, the key is to ensure that the benefit is both clear and relevant to the client and that the hassle of the engagement process is minimized for them. The financial cost (ie your fee) then becomes of less importance to the client in making their buying decision.

No two engagements will be alike because each client is different. To use the same structure (six one-hour sessions over four months for example) for all engagements will limit your success; flexibility is a requirement and allows you to minimize perceived hassle. A number of factors come into play for the client in assessing the 'hassle' element of this equation, including:

- The actual coaching process (eg 1:1 or in groups; the duration of each session; the frequency of sessions; the duration of the engagement etc).
- The time required (the sum of many of the above elements plus preparation and follow-up time).

- Whether the engagement will be face to face or by phone etc. (For example, a phone call requires little or no travel time to get to a meeting; if you agree to meet at the client's office they save time but you lose by the same token. Alternatively, the client may prefer to meet outside their office if they prefer to keep from their colleagues the fact that they are receiving coaching).

- Whether the engagement will be 1:1 or as part of a group (a 1:1 engagement is typically more intense and there is 'nowhere to hide' although the issues under consideration can be far deeper. However, it is arguable that a group session is more affordable, less 'threatening' and that the participants can learn from each other...).

- The amount of work required between sessions (in terms of embedding agreed changes to behaviour or to business practices).

- The nature of that work (and the degree of accountability enforced by the coach).

Some of those factors may also be presented as part of the benefits element. For example, if the coaching will be carried out as part of a group, the cost per person may be reduced (depending on how you set your fees). However, if the client has some personal issues on which they want to work this may prove harder in a group format.

As for the benefits element of the equation, once again several factors come into play that may not be obvious as client benefits. These could include:

- positive perceptions of you and your professionalism ('like and trust' and credibility);

- a clear understanding on the part of the client of the role you seek to fulfil for them;

- a feeling on the part of the client that they have been fully heard and that you are responding to specific issues that are important to them;

- the fact that:
  - not only does the client understand the benefits you will deliver and can visualize these, they also understand the results they can expect from taking part in this engagement and 'how it will feel' when they are successful;
  - the client feels that the benefits on which you focus are directly relevant to them;
  - the client believes that the results you promise are achievable and sustainable;
  - the solution you propose is broadly aligned with the solution that was already in the client's mind prior to your conversation.

Once again some of these factors may become relevant in the 'hassle' element of the equation; for example, you may demand more effort from the client than they feel able to give right now in order to achieve the desired results, or they may be fearful of a need to make permanent changes to behaviour patterns because it may in some way change 'who they are'.

As an example, a client of mine runs a weight-loss programme which is hugely successful in that his clients routinely lose considerable amounts of weight and they find that their bodies become more toned as a result of their work with him and the dietary changes he helps them put in place. However, towards the end of each programme, a large number of his clients ask when they can go back 'normal' eating and ease off on the exercise. He has to remind them that it was 'normal' eating combined with lower levels of exercise that brought them to him in the first place and that if they wish to maintain the weight loss they have achieved, their eating pattern will need to remain adjusted. In other words their current diet pattern (combined with maintenance of exercise) is now 'the new normal' for them.

Your information gathering process enables you to decide how to prioritize the data that the client provides, whether that is explicit or unconsciously.

Budget appetite

One more item of data that is invaluable to you and which can usually be gleaned only by asking a direct question is the budget appetite or availability of the client.

You may find that some potential clients are happy to meet with you in order to talk about their issues, in the context that you have set of a future coaching engagement. However, they may have no intention of paying for such an engagement. Instead they hope that the initial 'exploratory' meeting will give them some valuable insights or information and even that they may be able to stretch the 'free advice' into a second or subsequent meeting 'just to help me make up my mind...'. In short, there are people who will waste your time and act in a manner that is quite disingenuous in doing so.

This issue can be identified and resolved in part by the way in which you filter potential connections at the outset, partly by how you set up an initial meeting and in part by being quite open about the fact that you are running a business rather than a charity. One way to set expectations is to put up a section on your website about the fees you charge. Some coaches feel that this may act as a turn-off for potential clients. Others take the view that they prefer to talk about various fee options once they have had a conversation with the client so that they can present what seems to be the best engagement process option for that person, offer one or two alternatives and then relate the price of each to benefits delivered to the client.

My own website mentions fees obliquely with a statement to the effect that they are benchmarked against the typical billing rate for a partner in a City of London or Wall Street law firm. I adopted that approach to set a level of expectation but to allow me to flex the fee rate to reflect the nature and structure of the engagement under discussion, because no two engagements are alike and I prefer not to set fees based on an hourly or daily rate.

I also want to be able to charge a fee that reflects whether the individual is paying for my work with them out of their own pocket or if it is being paid for from a corporate budget. If the latter, I have no qualms about charging a full fee rate as the benefit of my work with the client will likely be felt across their firm as a whole and hence will impact the bottom line of the firm rather than simply being of help to the individual. If the client is paying for my services out of their own pocket I may well be happy to discount my normal fee rate or in some cases to work pro-bono. In part that decision will be based on the issues on which the client seeks help.

In a meeting with a client, at the point when we come to discuss the engagement I will usually ask a question along the lines: 'Do you have an idea of how you would like this engagement to work and also a budget in mind?' If the client is unable or unwilling to be clear on either point, I will then outline what I feel may be the best option for them, based on what they have told me up to that point and my typical fee rate for an engagement of that type. If the fee for that engagement pattern seems too high I will offer a different approach to the engagement and hence a lower overall fee level rather than simply discounting the fee rate.

Many coaches (especially in the United States) talk about the 'investment' that the client will have to make in order to work together. If you find this authentic and are comfortable to use this term, by all means do so. It certainly encourages a change of client view from cost to benefit.

Self-worth and confidence

In considering the value equation for your clients, you will also begin to develop your own sense of self-worth and the confidence to talk about value rather than simply focusing on the cost of your services. We look at this issue once again in Chapter 7 when considering fees and how to set them for your business. For now, have in mind that if you yourself have qualms about the value of what you deliver for clients, it is highly likely that this will come across in the way in which you talk about fees. In other words, if you don't fundamentally believe in the value of your services, neither will the client. The result will be either that the client goes elsewhere (because your hesitance conveys uncertainty and hence damages your credibility) or that you are pushed to lower your prices until you enter the 'profitless prosperity' trap. In thinking about how you articulate value to prospective clients, to combine a couple of advertising straplines may help to bolster your confidence in what you deliver and its worth to clients:

- 'Reassuringly expensive' (Stella Artois beer); and
- 'Because I'm worth it...' (L'Oreal hair care products).

In reinforcing your self-confidence in the value you deliver, keep in mind that the client is buying problem resolution and/or dream fulfilment. They do not usually care about how technically advanced your coaching may be nor yet about the process of coaching itself, or even if what you do is in fact more about mentoring, counselling or consulting. They do care about achieving results.

Building your value equations

Clearly, the value equation differs for each client – at least at the detail level. Many clients may have similar strategic issues that they seek to address and the likelihood of this is increased if your definition of your 'perfect' client is quite focused. You can save valuable time in meetings (and indeed avoid the need for a further meeting in some cases) by preparing some ideas in advance of typical value equations for your preferred clients.

I find that a good working model for this pre-preparation is to look at some typical 'commercial fit' issues that many clients seem to have and then to try and assess a cash or a 'soft' value on the resolution of those issues. I can then overlay additional data that come to light as a result of conversations with the client; for example, emotional drivers, learning preference, how they take buying decisions etc.

Similarly, if the commercial fit is around the fulfilment of a dream rather than resolving a problem, it can be fairly easy to assess the value to the client of enabling them to achieve their goals.

Of course, the 'benefit' to the client may well not be cash or bottom line focused. In addition, it is quite likely that you will not be able to help the client to resolve all of the issues that are raised in the 'commercial fit' context; indeed some of those issues may in fact be outcomes of success in other areas. The trick therefore is to focus on the issues where you can be of help (ie where the commercial fit is clear) and then ensure that you can assess value in terms that are relevant to the client – and which can be set in their mind against the cost of your services and the 'hassle' of the engagement process.

In the early stages of building your practice it may require some quite detailed questioning to understand what success would look like for a given client. In some cases, the end client may not be the primary buyer (the person who must actually take the decision to hire you and who has control over the budget). That is especially true in a business coaching context. In such cases you may need different value equations for each party – one for the end client and one for the primary buyer.

How might this work in practice? If we look at the '.50 calibre Barrett' referral example mentioned on page 99, the clear commercial fit was to enable the members of the investment banking team to identify and win larger deals than they had to date ('hunting elephants'). Following my initial meeting with the head of the team, I had a good idea of what that actually meant to him. In order that his team could be recognized as successful, they had, between them, to source and win two deals that positioned them as the lead adviser and generated revenue of $1 million or more. That had to be achieved within nine months in order that they could achieve their team goal for the financial year.

The main factor causing friction in achieving that clear goal was the lack of good enough relationships at a senior enough level with companies that could generate deals of that size. That, in turn, resulted from a combination of lack of confidence on the part of the individuals to approach suitable candidate firms at the appropriate level of seniority and (linked to that) a basic lack of network building activity; they simply were not making a sufficient number of calls to potential client firms. If I could enable each member of the team to change their approach to identifying and then initiating contact with appropriate potential client firms, there was a far higher likelihood that they would at least be on a shortlist of candidates to propose and then to advise on the deals such as mergers or acquisitions that might be done. The direct cash value to their firm of success in these aims was in excess of $2 million (two deals generating at least $1 million apiece). However, that outcome would be the result of building the confidence of the team as a whole that the target was achievable if each individual was willing to change their behaviours and do certain things differently. My focus in explaining how I might help this client was therefore on giving the team members a toolkit and methodology that would:

- help them to focus on client firms where there was a good potential fit;
- enable them to experience reduced stress in approaching such firms and setting up/running initial meetings with senior individuals within them;
- outline clear benefits to the leadership teams of those firms of working with them; and hence
- develop confidence in their ability to win lead advisory roles in the face of competition from much larger firms.

That example represents a fairly clear 'bottom line' based benefit to the client. In itself that would not necessarily get to a 'yes' decision for us to work together. If I could overlay some of the additional data that I gleaned from the conversation, so that I could use language that would resonate with the individual, it would be far more powerful. In this case, a clear emotional driver for the client was a combination of a need for recognition (ie being seen to be successful) combined with a strongly competitive streak in his character.

If I could talk in terms not simply of achieving targets but of 'winning' and 'killing the competition', those ideas would likely resonate, especially if I were to use visual language as he appeared to have a visual learning preference. It appeared that he was a strongly relationship-oriented buyer. It was therefore most helpful to go into the initial meeting on the back of a strong referral. However, it was necessary to take time to talk to the client about our common ground (in this case similar, though not shared, military experiences – without of course risking being seen to compete) and to extend that conversation into other areas such as sport, travel etc. The business element of the conversation was covered in less than 10 minutes out of a 50-minute meeting and the buying decision was essentially taken within the first 15 minutes – as is usually the case.

By contrast, if the client of a life coach is a working mother struggling to balance the demands of children and home as well as a job or running a business, the benefits she seeks will probably not be measured in cash terms. This client will be looking for reduced stress, a sense of being in control and of being able to fulfil all her chosen responsibilities to the level that she wishes whilst still having a life that she feels to be her own. Leaving aside the fact that she may need to have a job in order to balance the family finances as opposed to doing paid or unpaid work because it is stimulating, fulfilling etc, the issues here are not bottom line based but related to felt control and stress management.

The implied questions here in terms of the value equation are: 'What would the achievement of these aims be worth to you?' and 'How would you experience the benefits?' In order both to understand reality from the client's point of view and also to enable her to begin to experience what might be the results she can achieve with your help, you might want to ask exactly those questions if you feel it is appropriate to do so. This is in fact an extension of the information gathering approach that we explored in the previous chapter.

In order to articulate value most effectively we need to imagine something of the visceral frustrations or desires that have become a part of the client's life and hence the context for this engagement. The value you can deliver will be to alleviate those frustrations.

Articulating the value you deliver

Key ideas:

- clients will rarely if ever infer value; you always (in my experience) have to tell them explicitly the value you will deliver;
- clients rarely if ever buy coaching (or any other delivery process); they buy resolution of pain;
- clients always need to be able to answer in their own mind the question 'What's in this for me?' (and perhaps also 'What's in this for my team or those around me?').

With that in mind, most coaches struggle to articulate value because they focus on what matters to them – coaching and the coaching process. Coaching may well deliver benefits but if these are not aligned to benefits that are relevant to the client right now, they will not resonate and enable the client to say 'yes'.

In order to get over this problem, you will need to link:

- a key *idea* that is relevant to the client;
- the *benefit* you deliver to the client in relation to that idea; and
- the consequent *result* that the client will experience.

I think of this as a mnemonic: IBR – Idea, Benefit, Result.

For example, with the banker mentioned above:

I will enable each member of your team to adopt a methodical approach to identifying the right target clients. The benefit is that they will gain confidence with every call they make because they feel more in control. The result is that they will not waste time but will start to hammer your competitors and win more high-value business.

Or:

> I will enable you and your people to identify what factors drive each
> target client over and above pure commercial considerations. The
> benefit is that you will each be able to punch real hot buttons for the
> individual client. As a result your overall hit rate will go up markedly,
> you can win more business in the face of strong competition and you
> maximize profitability because you will avoid competing on price.

For the working mother struggling with conflicting demands, perhaps:

> I will enable you to identify what is most important for you (key idea)
> so that (benefit) you can give yourself permission to prioritize demands
> on your time and say 'no' to things that are apparently urgent but not
> important. As a result, you will feel more in control and experience less
> stress each day (result).

The word choice in each of these statements is important. Whether you
use the words idea, benefit and result is a matter of personal choice.
I find it helpful to do so as it directs the mind of the client accordingly.

Each statement should seek to combine a commercial fit issue with
words that touch emotional drivers for the particular client and also
seek to do so in a manner that feels authentic to you when you say it
out loud. By thinking about some examples in advance of your meetings, it will become easier to adjust the words you use to express a
given idea to the needs of a specific client. Ideally you will become
comfortable to do so 'on the hoof' in an initial meeting. The benefit
is to short-circuit the time required to win business with that client.
The alternative is to ask for a further meeting during which you can
'talk through' a proposal.

There may be occasions when that is necessary, and indeed you may
find it easier to go for this 'two-stage' approach so that you have time
to get your ideas in order, reflect on what you have learned in the
initial meeting and even put something in writing if you wish to do so
(or if the client asks you to do so). Over time, I have found that it is
more effective to be able to make a verbal statement of how I believe
I can deliver greatest benefit to the client during the initial meeting.

That may lead to a conversation about fees and budgets but more often than not the client will first give an agreement in principle that we should work together. Once we have that hurdle out of the way the fee discussion becomes easier as it is mostly a matter of tailoring the process of delivery so that it makes sense in terms of delivering the results the client seeks (ie the value of the engagement) at a cost they feel is sensible and in a manner that does not create too much friction or 'hassle'. By having a few generic 'IBR' statements in your head, you will have some starting points from which you will probably find it easier to craft something specific to the client across the table from you. In one case, it was necessary to go for a second meeting at which both the primary buyer and one of the end clients would be present. I prepared a document consisting of a three-column table, headed with the name of the firm and the division in which all of the end clients worked. Column 1 was headed 'Area of focus', Column 2 was headed 'Benefit that will be delivered' and Column 3 was headed 'Consequent outcome'. I added four rows below that, each outlining a particular issue (highlighted by the client in the initial meeting as a 'friction factor') would be addressed. In that second meeting, I explained that there were a couple of areas in which I could not help directly because the outcomes desired were in fact the result of success in other areas. I then placed the one page document in front of each person and kept silent as they read it. The response was to the effect that this was a complete solution and we should start work as soon as possible. Fees were mentioned only as an afterthought.

Handling competition

As coaches we always have competition. However, that competition is not always in the form of other coaches (whether external or in-house), in my experience. It may come in the form of alternative approaches to resolving the felt problem (a consulting exercise, some mentoring work, advice from a professional body etc). It may be something as basic as a conversation with a trusted friend or family member. It may indeed be the old and comfortable approach of 'do nothing'.

It is easy to become focused on competition and to seek ways in which you can prove that you are 'better'. In my experience that approach rarely succeeds because you can only influence issues that are directly under your own control. Clearly you must feel that you are capable of effective coaching and have the necessary training and knowledge. You must be comfortable that your fees reflect the value you deliver and feel comfortable to talk about them to potential clients. Competition is not normally an issue as such provided that you have engendered:

- basic 'like and trust';
- credibility in the eyes of the client (in the role that you seek with them);
- a sense that you have heard their issues at a deep level; and
- an understanding of the benefits you deliver.

As the father of an American friend of mine once said, 'There is no such thing as "the best restaurant", there's the one that that works best right here and now'.

In the case of business or executive coaching, selection onto a shortlist may be based on 'objective' factors. These might include items such as formal coaching qualifications, individual certification by an organization such as WABC or European Mentoring and Coaching Council (EMCC), the possession of additional educational qualifications such as an MBA or a diploma in psychology, accreditation as an Myers-Briggs Type Indicator (MBTI) or NLP practitioner etc. There may be additional factors such as foreign language capability, physical location, past business experience and level of seniority attained. You may decide that it is helpful to gain some additional qualifications in order to increase your chances of being shortlisted. However, once you are on the shortlist your ability to win business is once again down to the basic personal 'like and trust' perceptions you develop in that first meeting and your ability to build on these as outlined in this book.

There is therefore little point in focusing on what the competitors have that you don't. It is far more effective to focus simply on doing the work to:

- maximize the number of opportunities you have to connect with good potential clients for you;

- prepare for each client meeting as effectively as you can (and enable the client to prepare also by way of your pre-meeting e-mail or letter); and then

- simply be yourself and hold the best conversation you can.

If you focus on the competition it acts as a distraction.

There are two common reactions to competition:

1 reduce your price; and/or

2 find ways to 'knock' the competitor.

Neither is helpful. If you compete on price you simply devalue your own business both in the mind of the client and ultimately in your own mind; something that is deeply insidious as it undermines your self-confidence. If you 'knock' others you demean yourself. Not only do you fail to address any issues that may be in the client's mind, you may unintentionally raise issues because you create dissonance and a perceived lack of authenticity on your part.

In the next chapter we explore how to set your fees and do so in the context of the value that you deliver and also to talk about your fees to potential clients with a high degree of comfort on your part.

CHAPTER SUMMARY

- Potential clients become actual clients because they can (almost literally) see the benefits to themselves of your ideas and the value that you will deliver for them.

- Value can be defined as:

$$\frac{\text{Benefit (as defined by the client; rarely cash alone)}}{(\text{Cost} + \text{Hassle})}$$

- By simplifying the process of the engagement and being flexible about the process on a case-by-case basis, the perceived hassle is minimized. This needs to be reflected in the approach you adopt for fee setting.

- Clients will usually have in mind not only an outline of the solution they 'expect' to buy but also the price that they are willing to pay. If the benefits can be made clear and are greater than those the client expected, it is possible that the price they have in mind can be escalated.

- In some cases the budget is fixed. If so, adjust the process of engagement or the payment terms rather than simply reducing the fee.

- Decide whether to set expectations of fee levels on your website. Wherever you can, ask about budget appetite during your initial conversation. Otherwise outline what you see as the optimal engagement process for this client and why, plus what that would cost. If the fee is too great, ask what would be affordable and explain what can be done for that fee. Many coaches talk in terms of an 'investment' rather than a fee.

- It is important that you feel comfortable to talk about your fees and the value you deliver. If you are not robustly confident, it is hard to expect that the client will be.

- Think of a series of generic, linked 'idea, benefit, result' statements that can be adjusted 'on the hoof' to describe the value you deliver.

- Competition is a fact of life, but by no means always from other independent coaches. Other competitors may be in-house coaches, line managers or the old-fashioned 'do nothing' approach.

- There is no point in knocking competitors: it diminishes you.

- Clients will rarely (if ever) infer benefits; you must explain them explicitly.

Fees: how to be paid what you are worth

07

In the previous chapter we looked at the concept of value in the eyes of the client. This is a key element in setting your fees along with your confidence in the value that you deliver and your willingness to tell the client that explicitly. In order to be paid what you know you are worth you must be willing to say what that is and to stand by that when pressed to 'sharpen your pencil'. In this chapter we look at various different ways to determine what fee level you should set for yourself and expose the myth of the 'going rate'.

In short, there is no such thing as an overall 'going rate' for coaching any more than there is an overall going rate for legal fees. The rate charged by a senior partner in a City of London or New York law firm will differ considerably from those of a similarly senior person working for a small firm in a country town. Legal fees also vary depending on the nature of the work; for example a corporate lawyer will often charge more than one similarly qualified who handles family law matters such as divorce (although it may not seem that way to those involved!). The law practiced by the City lawyer and the person located in the small town is the same even if one has greater resources available than the other. The difference in fees is a combination of their actual cost of doing business and their positioning in the minds of clients. The latter is increasingly important in defining the fees chargeable by coaches. It is critical in maintaining high fee levels for some lawyers as clients look to results rather than to inputs such as the lawyer's time.

Much the same is true in the field of coaching. The reality is that fee rates vary widely, even within a given field of coaching such as business or executive coaching. The fee rates that you yourself can charge depend in my experience more on how you position yourself and your role with clients than on most other factors. Once again, therefore, much depends on your decisions about the kind of clients you prefer to work with, because another key factor is the budget availability of the type of individual you decide to target as your preferred client.

So, where do you start?

A reality check

As a first step, let's look at a basic reality check for your coaching business – which for the vast majority of independent coaches essentially means you. We look at some of the ways in which you can structure your business in Chapter 9. However, whether you work as an independent or as a member of a group of associates or in a more formal, corporate-type structure, your income will usually depend on the volume of coaching that you yourself carry out plus the degree to which you bring in those clients rather than have them handed to you. If you prefer not to win your own clients but to have them brought to you by others, be prepared to give up a large part of the fee that each client pays. With some of the coach broking firms that percentage can be anything from 20 per cent to (anecdotally) 60 per cent. That fee share may be a one-off or it may be for any engagement that you undertake with either the individual client or with the client firm, forever.

If we keep to an example of a lone, independent coach, with no other sources of income, the position is relatively simple. That person needs to bring in enough money to pay for their basic living costs such as housing, utilities, food, clothing etc, plus the cost of running their business, which might include fees paid to outsourced providers such as an accountant, but can be very low if need be. A checklist might look like Table 7.1 below:

TABLE 7.1   Personal costs to be considered

Item	Amount per month
Accommodation (rent + service charge or mortgage payment, plus maintenance costs of the property if you are liable for these)	
Council tax (Property tax in United States)	
Insurances (building, contents, personal, medical)	
Utilities (electricity, gas, water, sewerage, telephone, internet access)	
Food and drink (including items such as alcohol if required)	
Transport costs (car, or public transport costs). NB for car costs include not only any leasing payment or other purchase cost, but also insurance, tax, depreciation, servicing and fuel	
Clothing (one can of course survive for a time without buying new clothing but this is not possible longer term. This amount needs to cover both casual wear and business attire)	
Pet care costs if any	
Total	

In order to translate that into a base level fee rate, work out the number of hours you expect to coach and divide the total income needed by the number of hours... simple!

Actually no – it's not that simple.

The problem is that most coaches overestimate the amount of time that they expect to spend on coaching. That is often simple over-optimism. However, they also tend to underestimate the time required to run the business, carry out marketing and selling activities and do the necessary preparation for and follow-up after coaching sessions, which compounds the problem. The last two points are important because preparation and follow-up form part of the work that 'only you can do' – they are in fact just as much part of the coaching session as the face to face or phone to ear time with the client.

As a rule of thumb, therefore, for every hour of coaching delivery, add at least the same amount of spent time to cater for preparation and follow-up. Indeed, I typically reckon to add double the delivery time because of the nature of the work I do and the type of clients with whom I work. Therefore one hour of coaching requires three hours of what, to a lawyer or accountant, would be 'billable' time and what looks like a 90-minute session represents a half day's work.

Another factor that can skew the numbers is travel time. Many coaches do their work at the client's premises. Unless your clients come to you or you are coaching by phone or video conference system or similar, you need to allow for the time needed to reach the client and to travel between sessions. That is one of the reasons why you might be willing to offer a lower fee rate to a corporate client where you are working with more than one person in the firm and you can undertake several sessions on a given day.

A 'typical' working week

Clearly this depends in part on the amount of time you have spent as a coach and on building your business to date. The more experience you have the more likely it is that you will have a greater number of clients, that you will spend more hours actually coaching and that your fee rate per unit of time will be higher. That is certainly borne out by the most recent ICF survey. As a coach with a relatively new practice, the time allocation for a typical week might look something like:

- one day spent on administration, book-keeping, continuing professional development (CPD) and supervision; effectively running the business;

- one day spent on marketing activities including writing or otherwise developing collateral;

- one and a half days spent on sales development activities including network building;

- one and a half days spent on delivery for clients (ie coaching, preparation and follow-up, assuming that for each hour of delivery there will be one hour of preparation and up to one of follow-up, which may be tight).

Clearly it is possible to reallocate time from marketing activities to sales development and vice versa, and of course to treat preparation as a marketing activity; in other words there is flexibility here. It is also possible to add a sixth day to be used for follow-up or marketing activities etc. Indeed when I first started my own business I used to say that Sunday was sacrosanct and occurred once each week. However, that might sometimes be on a Wednesday. It is, however, a mistake to overcommit your time in starting and running a business, even when you may be doing something you love for the first time in your career. We explore time allocation in some detail in Chapter 11. However, for now, let's assume that you will operate on a five-day week (even if the days may be long).

If that broad outline above is even roughly accurate, it is clear that your coaching delivery time is unlikely to be more than say five or six hours a week, and your fee rate needs to reflect that. In addition, in my experience, few clients wish to work during the major holiday periods, which I think of as roughly two weeks either side of Christmas and during the month of August. That of course allows you to take holidays but also means that your chargeable time will occur over about 10 months each year. If that is the case then your fee rate needs to increase to reflect the reduced time over which your income requirement can be met.

To put this into context, if we assume that you wish to take as personal income £30,000 per year and we exclude tax, National Insurance and the cost to run the business such as professional fees, insurances etc, we can carry out a basic calculation using the other assumptions outlined above:

Gross revenue required: £30,000

Coaching hours available: 5 hours per week × 44 weeks = 220

Base fee rate: 30,000 / 220 = £136.36

However, this is only the start of the process and serves to give you a bare minimum fee level that will keep the wolf from the door. In addition, you need to allow for tax payable by the business (if it is a limited company), professional fees for accountancy and supervision, cost of professional association subscriptions, cost of insurances etc. A full checklist of costs might look like Table 7.2 below:

TABLE 7.2   Business costs to be considered

Allowance for corporation tax	
Payment of personal salary (and dividend if any) for owner	
Personal National Insurance (employment tax) for owner	
Personal pension contributions for owner	
Staff costs (including virtual assistant etc to cover salary/fee plus any added NI, pension and insurance costs)	
Office rent or use of virtual/serviced office	
Business rates (if applicable)	

TABLE 7.2 *continued*

Utilities (electricity, gas, water, sewerage, landline telephone (if any), internet access)	
Snack food and drinks (biscuits, coffee, bottled water etc)	
Transport to client meetings (public transport or business mileage on personal car – don't forget to tell your insurance company if you use your personal car for business)	
Client entertainment budget (coffee, lunches etc, if any)	
Technology (purchase and periodic replacement of computer, backup drive etc, mobile/cell phone)	
Website development, maintenance and hosting	
CPD/training/supervision	
Membership of professional bodies/certification	
Business insurance (including liability, buildings etc plus perhaps critical illness etc)	
Accountancy, legal and other professional services	
Regulatory returns/filing fees (eg annual return to Companies House for limited companies, Data Protection registration)	
Total	

Clearly you can play with the numbers and make any set of assumptions you feel reasonable. You can decide to pay others to do more of the non-core work by outsourcing. You can extend your working days (but only to a degree if the business is to be sustainable). You can work weekends (again only to a degree and only for so long). The point is that you get to charge a fee (in most cases) only when you are actually coaching. The result of fee rate times hours coached determines your income – unless you use a different structure as we examine below.

Time is your only asset. Whilst I do not recommend that you sell time to clients as such, I highly recommend that you calculate and attribute a realistic value to your time and that you take account of what a lawyer would consider 'billable hours' over and above the actual time spent in a session. Only then can you know what it will cost you to deliver a coaching engagement.

Rather than looking at the number of coaching hours available, another approach is to think instead of the number of clients you expect to work with at any given time. You can then decide on the number of sessions per month and the duration of each session. It would be a mistake, however, to expect the number of hours of delivery time to go up radically in your first year or so of practice. Thereafter you can probably outsource more non-core work such as administration and maintenance of collateral material in order to win more billable work. In terms of fee rates you charge, the result of any time-based approach is likely to be similar.

The essential lesson is that undercharging is a very short route to either bankruptcy or to taking a job to pay the bills whilst you use your free time to build a coaching business (or you treat coaching as a paying hobby). Sadly too many good coaches appear to do just that.

Fee structures

So far we have focused on minimum fee levels that ensure you can survive. You still need to win the work and do all the other things that go to ensure the success of your business. How might we structure the fees so that:

- they are perceived to be affordable for clients;
- they deliver a reasonable level of income/profit for you as the coach and (if possible); and
- they do not limit you to the slavery of the billable hour?

There are many ways in which you can set fees. However, it is important to be able to offer a given client more than one option so that (assuming you want to work with that person) you can ensure that there is a viable way for you to work together. You can achieve this by tailoring the nature and/or pattern of the engagement so that the fee becomes affordable rather than either discounting price or losing the business entirely. Approaches to fee setting include:

- per hour;
- per session;
- a fee for a set engagement (eg nine sessions of one hour each over six months with a 15-minute phone call between sessions);
- results-based fees.

Other options could include variations in the process of the engagement, such as:

- solo engagement versus group format (so that costs can be shared between participants);
- face to face versus sessions by telephone or video conference (you save travel time and costs if you do not need to meet at a client's premises);
- fees that include or exclude expenses.

I prefer to avoid fees based on a per-hour or per-day rate. From the client's perspective I feel it sends a signal that I am selling an input (my time) rather than an output (results for the client). This approach also means that, in the client's mind, the 'meter is running' every time they feel a need to pick up the phone to me between sessions and so they will be less inclined to do so, which may impact the results that can be achieved. Separately, although there is more to do in most sessions than there is time available, I have had clients for whom a highly focused 30–40 minutes delivers tremendous value even if we have booked a session lasting 90 minutes. If we work on a time spent basis I cannot recycle that time. In other words the 'meter running' argument can cut both ways unless you are working on a total fee for an engagement rather than per hour.

A per session fee is fine and indeed I have had several client firms ask for a per session fee rate over the last couple of years given that the firm has no way of knowing if the redundancy axe will fall on any given individual within the coming few weeks, let alone over the period of a six- or twelve-month engagement. In such cases, I sometimes agree that I will continue to work with the individual on career transition issues if they are made redundant and that this will trigger automatically a new, mini-engagement paid for by the firm as part of the redundancy package. Clearly if the client wishes to continue beyond that mini-engagement we have another conversation.

In the past I would usually win engagements based on a block of six or twelve months. We would agree an expectation of the number of sessions and the duration of each session at the outset. I would undertake to provide unlimited access (within reason) by way of e-mail or phone between sessions during normal business hours. In reality it was rare for that option to be used by clients unless in an emergency. I would invoice 50 per cent of the fee at the start of the engagement with the rest on a quarterly basis.

Today, very few engagements are for periods longer than six months and three months of focused work is far more common. In many more cases there is a discussion at the outset about specific results. In the past, even though I always asked about such measures before starting an engagement, it was sometimes hard to gain any real clarity. In terms of billing cycles, I still ask for 50 per cent of the fee up front even for a three-month engagement with the remainder paid either monthly or quarterly, depending on the duration of the engagement agreed. In such situations I rarely offer a 'break' clause in the agreement and certainly not for an engagement of less than six months.

In the past, I have been asked on several occasions about results based fees; for example enabling a banker or partner in a law firm to win a specific deal with a low basic fee to cover costs and a 'success' fee that was far higher if the deal was done. In the event, not one of those deals was ever finalized. The main reason was that, in each case, it would have been hard to calculate the actual results achieved until long after the event.

For example, it is one thing for a law firm to win the lead adviser role on something like a major infrastructure project, it is another thing to know what the fee revenue will be until the project has been delivered, which might be several years down the line. In one case the fee arrangement that was contemplated was not one that the organization was, ultimately, willing to honour. When it became clear that the sum on which my small percentage would be based might be large enough that the value of the fee would have been measured in many tens of thousands of dollars, it proved, unsurprisingly, to be unfeasible for the firm in question.

If you are willing to consider a results-based fee, it is vital to ensure that the results required are clear before the engagement begins, that they are readily measurable, that there is a well-documented contractual arrangement between the parties and that both sides are willing and able to deliver against it. Don't forget that a contract is worth only as much as the lengths to which you are willing to go in enforcing it and that there is indeed such a thing as a pyrrhic victory in legal conflicts.

Actual fee levels

In our example above we looked at a way to come up with a quick and dirty calculation of your basic fee level; one that would cover your minimum income needs. In reality you need to be more sophisticated than that and it is essential that you know with a fair degree of certainty what it costs you to live and also what it costs you to run your business. You also need to know which of these costs are fixed and which are variable. For example, if I outsource book-keeping to my accountant I gain immediately in terms of time saved, but there is an almost equally immediate cost increase for the business. If I must travel to the client's office for sessions, I need to factor in the time taken and the cost of travel. These can be significant if, as I have done, you travel overseas for some engagements, which will usually require at least one night at a hotel.

As mentioned above, under-charging is a sure and potentially rapid way to bankruptcy. In order to be able to set your fees for any given pattern of engagement, you must know what it will cost you to deliver that engagement. That plus the amount of your income requirement that you attribute to the engagement is the base fee below which you must not go.

Fee levels vary widely

For most coaches, especially those starting out, there may be a lack of confidence to talk to clients about what might seem on the face of it to be large figures in terms of fees. That can be compounded by the fact that there is not a huge amount of concrete data around on fee rates unless you spend time looking at the websites of other coaches in your geographic area and in your field of coaching – and by no means all such websites will quote fees. When fee levels are quoted, the variations can be significant. One US-based coach (Michelle Schubnel in her blog at **www.coachandgrowrich.com**) quotes the following fee bands:

- life coaching: $200–$750 per month;

- business coaching: $350–$2,500 per month;
- executive coaching: $500–$5,000 per month.

In a January 2009 report published in *Harvard Business Review*, the median fee rate for business coaching was found to be approximately $500 per hour but with a low figure of $200 per hour ranging up to a high figure of $3,500 per hour. By contrast, a report published by the Association for Coaching in 2004 (which still appears on their website, **www.associationforcoaching.com** at the time of writing) quoted fees of £50–£75 per hour rising to £125–£250 per hour in the context of business coaching. The latter equates to roughly $200–$400 per hour at current £/$ exchange rates. Allowing for inflation since 2004 that ties in broadly with the most common band of target fee rates, based on responses to a survey that I ran in the second half of 2012 where most of the respondents (80 per cent) were business coaches, which was between $300 and $400 per hour.

The 'going rate'? Pick a number...

You may wish to set more than one rate per coaching hour depending on factors such as whether the client is paying for an engagement out of their own pocket or the fees are to be paid by their firm. You may want to set a lower rate for work with charities/not for profit organizations or for work in specific sectors such as education. If you do so, then (a) you will need to set a limit on the volume of such discounted fees in the context of your overall income needs; and (b) it is important that you are clear in your own mind as to why you make that choice and that you are able to explain to the client why they are offered a rate that is lower than your norm.

There is of course a possible issue of being considered discriminatory. However, one of the joys of running your own business is that you choose with whom you work and you may feel that you prefer not to accept an engagement with a potential client that raises this sort of point.

Keep in mind that it is hard to raise fee rates once you start working with a given client. If, for example, you work with a client who pays out of their own pocket for a series of sessions at a reduced rate and then changes role, moving into a corporate environment, it will be hard to win a fee increase unless you have been explicit at the start that you will increase fees as and when they change role.

In terms of talking about your fees, preparation helps to raise your level of confidence, even to the extent of rehearsing your answer to the obvious question: 'How much do you charge?'

It is possible that 'sticker shock' will occur no matter what your fee rate is, unless expectations are set before you begin a concrete discussion on costs. Some coaches list fees on their websites. That can be a two-edged sword; putting off some clients from entering a conversation in the first place before they begin to understand the value you deliver but also avoiding wasted time and effort in discussions with potential clients who will never have available the sort of budget needed to work with you under any circumstances. Fee listings on websites also reduce your flexibility to tailor fees to a level that is appropriate to the engagement pattern you agree to undertake.

I recommend making a list of key points that can help you to head off 'sticker shock' on the part of clients. For example:

- an hour of coaching represents three hours of elapsed time – so your fee rate represents only a 33 per cent billing level;
- your fee covers expenses and travel time, not just delivery;
- (in a business or executive coaching context) if an hour of your time is not worth at least the same as an hour of the client's time why would the client hire you?;
- if you do not charge a reasonable fee you go out of business;
- 'buy cheap, buy twice'.

I have seen some coaches adopting a common marketing practice – especially in online transactions – known as 'risk reversal'. This is in effect a guarantee that, if the promised value is not achieved the client's money will be refunded. I feel that this is not a good idea, partly because it feels 'tacky' to me in this context but more importantly because the coach cannot actually control the achievement of the required results. Much of that is down to the efforts of the client and the degree to which they engage in the coaching process and take action as a result. Once you have spent time in coaching sessions, it is gone. To return fees due to factors that are typically hard to measure, where measurement is often subjective and which are outside your direct control is not a great idea for the health of your bank account. In addition, this approach encourages you to own the results to be achieved whereas the essence of coaching is that the ownership sits with the client.

A 'retainer' fee approach, which allows both parties to terminate an engagement at no notice and without penalty and with no further financial commitment, is often helpful, however.

Engagement structures

We look at the structure of coaching engagements in more detail in Chapter 8.

The structure of an engagement is what may allow you to bridge a budget gap by bringing together a client's aspirations, your revenue requirements and a satisfactory (if not an ideal) coaching process. By offering a variety of structures, you can create a tiered approach to pricing which:

- allows a client to 'try before they commit' with a lower priced approach;
- may reduce perceived risk in the eyes of the client of them making a poor buying decision; and
- maximizes the probability that the client can find a way to work with you that they perceive to be affordable.

In many cases an initial 'baby steps' engagement will lead on to something larger once the client becomes comfortable that you do indeed deliver the value that you promised; in other words that they are seeing a good return (in whatever form they choose to measure it) on their investment. This type of tiered approach has been used successfully by many types of business ranging from supermarkets (Essentials, Everyday Value, Finest) to car makers offering different trim levels on the same model, to gym memberships (off-peak, daytime only, any time).

Rather than offering a whole gamut of packages and prices and asking the client to choose one, I suggest that you determine the results the client seeks to achieve and, of those, what you can reasonably deliver, plus the client's budget appetite before you begin to discuss fees. By doing so, you can focus your offering on a small range of options, not more than three and preferably only two, which makes the choice easier. The fee conversation then becomes:

> Ms Client, based on what you have told me and the results you are
> looking to achieve, I feel that the best structure for our work together
> would be [outline the process]. My fee for that type of engagement is
> [£xxxx]. How does that sound to you?

This approach not only makes a clear recommendation but links explicitly in the client's mind the value they expect to receive and the financial cost. If the client says that the fee is more than they hoped to pay, you can ask questions to clarify what figure would be feasible and adjust accordingly. However, what you adjust should be the process of the engagement rather than the fee rate per coaching hour. You are selling value in the form of results but the cost to deliver is based on the finite asset of your available time.

Options for structuring engagements could include:

1 single session;

2 package of a set number of sessions delivered over a fixed period (eg six sessions over six months);

3 package of a set number of sessions delivered within a limited time frame (eg five sessions delivered during a nine-month period at times to be agreed);

4 as for 3 but with support by phone or e-mail between sessions;

5 open-ended engagement based on a retainer fee with sessions at pre-arranged periods (eg monthly, bi-weekly);

6 as for 6 but with support between sessions;

7 any of the above with a choice between 1:1 or group format;

8 any of the above with delivery by phone, video conference or Skype.

Of these, the single paid-for session is really an extension of an initial chemistry meeting (for which few coaches charge in my experience and for which most clients do not expect to pay). It can also be a good way to help a client you already know to navigate through a specific issue. Some coaches offer a free session to allow the client to experience at first-hand what it will be like to work together and the depth of the coaching conversation.

The 'six sessions over six months' approach has become a default norm in the field of business coaching. Six months is long enough to deliver meaningful results and for behavioural change (if required) to be observed and cemented. Much more than one session per month can become claustrophobic for both client and coach and there can be too little achieved between more frequent sessions to produce observable change. In the changed business environment, post the financial crisis that started in 2008, I find that many executives perceive themselves to be too busy to make time for coaching and also wish to see immediate results. I have therefore added a 'short, sharp' engagement of four one-hour sessions delivered at a rate of one per three weeks to my armoury, which has proved to be quite popular.

As a rule, I always include reasonable access between sessions by phone or e-mail. The reason is simply that life is rarely smooth and issues will arise between session times that are likely to be several weeks apart. To deny a client access between sessions is likely, in my view, to damage the relationship that has taken so much effort to establish and which is vital to the success of the coaching process. From the client's point of view, they know that they can pick up the phone when they need to do so. However, I have never (yet) had a client abuse that privilege.

Charging for expenses

I also include expenses in my fee rate where possible. I find that this saves a huge amount of time haggling over minor costs. It also obviates any issues of budget over-run. The majority of my clients are currently based within a 30-minute walk of my office. The expenses associated with an engagement will therefore be minimal.

Where I travel within Western Europe, I have hitherto been able to agree fees that are sufficient to cover expenses. For travel outside Western Europe, I usually ask that the client covers reasonable travel costs (air fare and a moderate hotel). In many such cases the client makes the travel arrangements and I find that they are more lavish than I would have chosen for myself. However, that does limit my flexibility in (for example) adding a couple of days to a business trip to do some sightseeing in a location that I might not otherwise visit. The key issue in deciding whether to take on work in distant locations is time and whether you will realistically be able to use the travel time for things such as writing, reading professional journals etc. If so it is not dead time.

Group sessions

Group sessions are a good way in which to allow clients to spread cost so that it becomes more affordable per person. Clients can also learn from each other although it is essential that there is a good level of trust between the participants at the outset, and issues may arise that need to be handled 1:1, so the engagement structure and fee arrangements may need to be flexible and contracting will be complex. Group sessions are tough to run; it is not unlike playing two or three games of chess simultaneously. However, I find them hugely stimulating if tiring.

I find that it helps to have a flip chart available during these sessions because it helps to keep track of things such as individual goals and actions agreed. It is also helpful if there is a point of conflict to ask the relevant individual to (for example) write in bullet point form their concerns on the flip chart. The conversation can then focus on what is written, which tends to direct negative energy to the flip chart rather than to people who may or may not be present. When actions are agreed, I often ask each person to write out their actions on a separate flip chart sheet and, when they are done, to sign the sheet, psychologically reinforcing their commitment. It can then be pinned up in their office as a reminder. I ask that they type up the action list and e-mail it to me and to the others present, which further reinforces the commitment.

'Remote' coaching

In terms of 'remote' delivery using phone, video conference or something like Skype, this can be highly efficient as it reduces travel time for one or both parties and costs can therefore be reduced to a degree. I find it less effective than a face-to-face engagement, however, and prefer to limit phone calls etc to support between sessions. I also find it harder to coach without the para-language that one receives in a face-to-face meeting; it is not impossible but it makes the coaching process harder in my experience.

I have, however, come across some coaches who offer not only 'remote' coaching but remote group coaching. This can certainly reduce cost, but to my mind this is likely to be not much more effective than a webinar in terms of delivering individual value. It may be helpful for some clients and it is certainly a good way for a coach to leverage their available time. I confess that I have never attempted to provide coaching in this way so my scepticism is based only on personal prejudice.

Terms and conditions

Much is written in coaching literature about contracting. It seems to me that there are two levels of contracting. On one hand there is the mechanical 'stuff' about fees and payment terms, the outline process of engagement and the boundaries of the engagement (which some people think of in terms of the role of the coach and not straying beyond the bounds of relevant expertise; for example into areas that would be better addressed by a psychologist or even a psychiatrist). On the other there are the arguably more important but 'softer' issues such as confidentiality, feedback loops, definition of success etc. Neither of these covers the setting of goals for individual sessions, which in my experience is always best done at the start of the session, recognizing that even then the goal may change during the session as a result of the coaching process.

In general I do not use a formal contract as such. I do write a letter to the client and to the primary buyer (if that is a different person) confirming the agreement we have reached by way of the results being sought, the mechanism for feedback, confidentiality and fee arrangements. That letter also refers to a set of terms and conditions that cover mechanical issues such as (in no particular order):

- cancellation terms (to cover missed or postponed sessions);
- if you are certified by an organization such as WABC, ICF etc then a statement of that fact, the fact that you are therefore bound by their ethics policy and a note of where that policy can be viewed (ie the website);
- a statement to the effect that you will maintain confidentiality as agreed with the client and confirmed in your letter of engagement, subject to a requirement under a court order to disclose information or to becoming aware of what appears to be illegal activity such as money laundering;
- fee payment terms such as timing of payments (which are stated on each invoice), including interest chargeable on late payments if that is the case; and
- issues of liability.

The last is important, in particular if you carry professional indemnity insurance. If that is the case, it may be helpful to state the amount of your cover and which company underwrites the policy and to indicate that the policy conditions are available on request.

If possible, keep your terms and conditions to a single sheet of paper. If you write your confirmation letter (your 'Letter of Engagement') well, it can normally be kept to two or three sides of paper at most with the T&Cs as an Appendix.

In some cases, the client will ask for a detailed description of your engagement process. If you offer a variety of engagement patterns as outlined above, this can be tough because each might be different. In practice the number of variations is not huge and you can prepare a series of outlines covering each possible pattern by describing each element in isolation and simply copying and pasting them together as a description of the specific engagement in hand. Obviously you will need to proof-read that description carefully.

Payment terms

My own payment terms are simple:

- In most engagements, I invoice 50 per cent of the total at the outset, with the remainder payable on a quarterly basis, spread evenly over the remainder of the engagement. The exception is where I agree a retainer fee, which is usually paid monthly. In some cases, I invoice the first three months' fees up front and move to monthly payments thereafter. If I have agreed a retainer fee, I typically invoice monthly because although it entails a slight administrative hassle it avoids any need to issue credit notes for fees that are no longer due if the engagement is stopped earlier than expected. (That also avoids issues of VAT refunds, which can be interesting.)

- Fees are payable within 30 calendar days of the date of the invoice and I state that settlement date on the invoice (making sure that it does not fall on a public holiday or a weekend). In my T&Cs I reserve the right to charge interest on late payments. I now use a level of 10 per cent per annum, calculated daily or 5 per cent above the base rate of HSBC, whichever is the higher. I have never made use of that provision in practice but it does set expectations.

Occasionally, I have encountered client companies that operate a 60- or even 90-day payment policy in respect of all payments to what they think of as 'suppliers'. If you accept a 90-day payment pattern you will, even if the invoice is paid on time, be subsidizing that firm's cash flow over that period and for a newly established coach that may mean that you carry a higher personal credit card balance for that period. I have three approaches to this type of situation:

- Ask the primary buyer to authorize an exception to standard policies. If the person in question is sufficiently senior that is not usually a problem.

- Invoice the whole fee up front (which works for a six-month or longer engagement as you will be paid in full roughly half way through).

- Increase the invoice by an amount that reflects the notional loss of interest on the money and accept the extended payment period.

It is important that you chase up late fee payments promptly. The longer you leave a fee outstanding the less likely it is to be paid. This is simply good business practice and does not need a heavy-handed approach, certainly not in the first instance. In most cases a phone call or a short, friendly e-mail to the client to say that the payment against your last invoice does not seem to have crossed your bank statement; it may have been misdirected by the bank so could they please confirm the payment details so you can follow it through will do the trick. I have very rarely had to chase an invoice more than once. In the cases where it has become an issue, I have proposed to invoice up front in future or simply refused to continue the engagement until the invoice has been settled.

Failure to chase payments can backfire. In one case, a client wound up one company and started another due to changes in his business model that I had enabled him to make. Some six months later my accountant drew to my attention the fact that a (thankfully quite small) invoice was outstanding from over nine months before. The company to which I had sent that invoice no longer existed. Game over. Prompt chasing up of late payments also avoids the problem of firms closing off their books at a year-end and being unwilling either to revise their accounts or to make a payment from the current year's budget, especially if no budget now exists for coaching.

The relationship pyramid

This is a simple concept that enables you to consider the level of your relationship with the client and hence (within reason) the elasticity of your fees.

This is linked somewhat with the way in which buying decisions are taken which we explored in Chapter 5. The pyramid (see Figure 7.1) helps you to look at the nature of your relationship with a client (past or current) through the eyes of the client. It can help you – in the light of an initial meeting – to decide to what level you can reasonably expect to take the relationship over the duration of your engagement.

FIGURE 7.1   Relationship pyramid 1

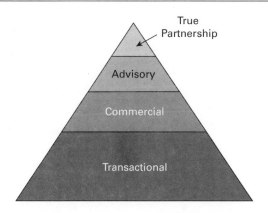

The bands within the pyramid indicate not only the level of the relationship but the percentage of clients that you might expect to find at that level of relationship based on the relative size of the band.

At the base of the pyramid, we have transactional relationships. Many clients in the fields of IT, engineering and procurement will naturally fall into this band. Their focus is on speed of delivery, measurable results and price. They do not always relate the price to the value of the results. In order to succeed with this type of relationship you will need to help them understand at each step of the journey why you are doing something, the benefit to them and then relate that to a measurable output. At a fairly early stage of the engagement, the client should be able to 'see' that they have already gained value relative to the fee paid. Nonetheless they may still press you on cost.

At the next level up, we have commercial relationships. At this level, price is still an issue but the client generally 'gets it' in that they understand what you expect to enable them to do differently or better, that there is a measurable value in that for them and that the value is not necessarily in pure cash terms; 'feeling less stress' is valuable even if it does not add directly to the bank balance. Price (fee level) is still an issue for commercial clients but is not the primary driver of their decisions. In other words they will not go for a cheaper quote automatically as a transactional buyer will. So long as they basically like you and feel that you understand their issues and can help to resolve them they will work with you satisfactorily. They do, however, seek results in short order and hence the duration of engagements may need to be shorter. If you can remind them along the way of the value you have delivered so far and of the end goal and you can reinforce the fact that the goal is achievable, these clients will be fine and will probably re-engage you at some point in the future. Their focus is on 'What's in it for me?' Fee levels can be reasonably elastic so long as you link the benefits/value clearly to results at the end of the engagement. Positive reinforcement is essential.

Above the commercial relationship comes that of advisory. This may develop during an extended engagement but may not become apparent until the client approaches you to re-engage. At this point, the nature of the conversation changes. It will typically become more strategic and will only dip into tactical issues, although often at great depth. You have become the client's 'go to' person in a specific field and they will often call on your advice outside any formal engagement structure. If this is reasonably infrequent you may want to help simply to keep the relationship warm. If the frequency of informal contact becomes oppressive, it may be time to talk about an ongoing retainer fee. You may also have the opportunity to raise the level of relationship to that of true partnership.

As the size of this tip of the pyramid indicates, these relationships are few and far between. They can be a two-edged sword. On the one hand they serve to lock out competitors (including that most insidious competitor of all, 'do nothing'). On the other, they can be very time consuming to maintain so you will need to ensure that the benefits to you of raising a given relationship to that status justify the ongoing time and effort and, frankly, that you enjoy the relationship at a personal level sufficiently to choose to spend time with the individual as much as a friend as a client. We look at this in more detail in Chapter 10, where we explore strategic client leadership.

Partnerships stem from your proven capability to make a huge, positive difference to the client by enabling them to resolve significant issues successfully and/or to fulfil certain deeply felt aspirations. At this level you become the person to whom the client turns for advice in any area of business or personal life where they experience friction. This requires that you are clear in your own mind about the boundaries of your technical knowledge and experience and know when to advise the client to speak to an expert in the relevant field. If you are able to recommend a credible expert, so much the better. These partnership relationships are incredibly valuable. They can result in excellent referrals as well as long-term and expanding client relationships. Price is a minor issue in such relationships but it behoves you not to milk that fee cow too hard because to do so risks damaging the relationship.

For such relationships to be successful, the client must continue to see you as a critical pathway to their own success and as someone who can be trusted to have to interests of the client at the top of your agenda at all times. To ask for a fee rate that could be seen as excessive risks early termination of the relationship even though you win the engagement. How do you know when you have a partnership? The client will talk to you about personal issues, family problems, concerns about their children and deep strategic and people issues to do with their business. They will not need you to prime them with questions; the occasional nudge will be enough. They will know how your mind works and will often answer questions that you might have asked without the need for you to do so.

In addition to providing you with referrals, this type of relationship may well offer you the opportunity to refer trusted colleagues to that client firm. Do not do so lightly! To develop such relationships takes time and it would be unlikely that it can be achieved in much less than a year to 18 months. They can be broken in moments: handle with care!

In the next chapter we look at how to organize the coaching process for success, including how to write excellent proposals (or letters of confirmation) which may be necessary in the case of a complex sale involving several buyers.

CHAPTER SUMMARY

- There is no such thing as a single 'going rate' for coaching. Fee levels vary widely, with executive and business coaching fees typically much higher than those for life coaching and other coaching disciplines.

- Many coaches underestimate the fee level they must charge in order to make a living and by the same token overestimate the amount of time that they will actually spend on coaching.

- There is also a tendency to underestimate the cost of running the business and the impact on available coaching time of factors such as preparation and follow-up.

- The latter will typically be at least the same as the delivery time and often twice as much, so that one hour of coaching will occupy two to three hours of 'billable' time.

- Fee structures need to balance perceived affordability for the client (and be perceived to deliver good value), with a reasonable level of profit/income for you whilst not tying you to the slavery of the billable hour.

- In order to set fee levels, you need to know how much an hour of your time must be worth. However, charging by the hour is usually a source of unnecessary friction in engagements. A fee for the overall engagement or a retainer fee will often give a better answer for both sides.

- Where practicable, it serves to minimize friction and scope for unhelpful negotiation if your fee includes expenses.

- Before offering a fee proposal, try to ascertain the client's budget appetite. (It allows you to adjust the structure of the engagement rather than the fee rate more easily: see Chapters 8 and 9.)

- Your terms and conditions ('T&Cs'), combined with any written proposal or letter of confirmation represent a good way to ensure that your fees are paid and paid on time. The T&Cs should cover issues such as cancellation and postponement of sessions as well as payment terms.

- The level of your relationship with the client (in terms of the relationship pyramid) tends to determine the elasticity of your fee rates.

- The structure of a coaching engagement (for example 1:1 versus a small group or face-to-face versus remote coaching by telephone) can be a major factor in the fee level that is achievable and also the profitability of the engagement for you.

Structuring and delivering a successful coaching engagement

08

There are several ways to define 'success' in a coaching engagement. Clearly the primary factor is the delivery of results that represent success for the client. In addition, however, success can also reflect:

- the degree to which the client and the coach form a strong connection on a business and/or personal level;
- the likelihood that the client will refer the coach to others;
- the willingness of the client to act as a reference for the coach;
- the degree to which the coach wishes to find additional ways to work with the client and/or to extend the engagement;
- the degree to which the client becomes an advocate of coaching as a development approach for others in their business and/or professional network.

All of these results are connected and are in large measure the result of the way in which you design and deliver the coaching process. That does not mean 'Did you, in each session, follow the GROW model rigorously?' – nor yet 'Did you use GROW or any other model?' The focus here is on the structure of the engagement as a whole and how you adjust the flow of the engagement to ensure that the outcomes achieved are as positive as possible for the client and also for your relationship with them. In this chapter we look at each step of the process and highlight the main success factors at each stage.

We begin with the initial 'chemistry' meeting, which may well be the first occasion on which you meet the end client.

The chemistry meeting

It may be that your chemistry meeting occurs after you have written a proposal or letter of some kind confirming your fees etc. That is more likely where you are being hired by a primary buyer who is not the end client but may be, for example, the HR director of an organization. The chemistry meeting is likely to be your first real interaction with the client unless that client is also the primary buyer. Either way it will determine whether or not you will end up working together and indeed the first few minutes will be critical.

I recommend that you handle a chemistry meeting exactly as you would any other initial meeting (see Chapter 5). It must be planned: use the meeting planner. It is an information gathering meeting so it will be helpful – indeed necessary – to send a pre-meeting e-mail or letter confirming the logistics, outlining your aim and the results you seek, and preparing the ground by posing a question or two to kick-start the conversation. As you arrive at the client's office, relax so that you can be yourself. Once the introductions are made and coffee poured, repeat verbally your aim and the results you seek. The client will almost always nod and say 'yes'; ask if the client has had a chance to read your e-mail and think about your question(s); get the client to talk through their answers.

Clearly the aim of a chemistry meeting is for the client to get to know you to a degree. By all means interact as the client talks about themselves and answers your questions. The idea is not to remain stoically silent but to encourage the client to do most of the talking. The more they talk the more information you gain, and the easier it becomes to articulate benefits you can deliver that are relevant to the client and expressed in language that resonates with them. However, it is highly likely that the client will at one point ask about your experience, your background, your family etc.

That is probably not the moment to tell your entire life history from birth to date. Pre-select a few personal and career highlights that are relevant to the client if you can. Otherwise offer the bare outline of your CV with, at each key stage, an indication of what caused you to make a change of direction (if that is what occurred) or what you delivered that made that role successful for you and/or for your employer. If it seems to be relevant by all means mention items such as education and your coach training. In most cases, if the client wants to know where you went to school or even to university they will ask. Your coach training might be a necessary box to tick – again if asked – in which case you might well mention individual certification and/or membership of professional organizations. If you have chosen not to become certified in your own right you might use this opportunity to outline why, thereby pre-handling a potential objection to hiring you. By and large, I would wait to be asked about certification rather than raise the issue, mainly because in my experience it comes up rarely in such conversations.

By all means mention family and outside interests if you feel it is appropriate. It may well be essential if the client is a relationship-oriented buyer (as outlined in Chapter 5). Be aware that your chosen hobbies or sporting pursuits might send signals that may be seen as negative and that some clients may have strongly-held views on issues such as hunting or gun ownership. You may therefore want to think twice about mentioning your love of clay shooting or even of fishing, for example. Both may be considered by some to be blood sports, even if on the basis of a misconception. Indeed a guest at a dinner party reacted badly when it was mentioned that I shot clay pigeons. She felt that wild pigeons were fast and agile enough to have some chance of evading the shot. However, to slow them down with balls of clay round their feet was decidedly unsporting.

Keep to time during the chemistry meeting and keep the meeting reasonably brief. It sends a signal that you respect the time of the client as well as your own and sets up a professional approach for the engagement as a whole. I try hard not to go beyond 45 minutes for a chemistry meeting. By that time the client has long made their decision one way or the other (indeed it will probably be made within the first 10–15 minutes of the meeting). Before you make ready to leave, do ask if the client has other questions for you and confirm that they feel happy to work with you, all other things being equal. Agree specific 'next steps' rather than leaving them in the air. You are in effect confirming that the engagement can go ahead so far as the end client is concerned.

It may be that the client will be asked by the primary buyer/HR director to meet more than one coach. If that is the case and they have others to see they will not be able to confirm that you will be their final choice. They will almost certainly know by the end of the meeting if they do not wish to work with you. A light-touch confirmation question allows them to tell you so in a manner that is non-threatening to them. If the client says 'no' then by all means ask if there is a particular reason; it is good feedback. However, do not press the point unless there is a mechanical objection such as budget or timing that can be overcome simply by adjusting the process of engagement. To be seen as pressuring the client will do you no good in the event that you may have other opportunities with the same organization.

It should be rare for you to go into a chemistry meeting without the client expecting that they would be willing to work with you, provided that your pre-qualification of the 'fit' has been effective. An exception is where there is a visceral dislike, which you will almost certainly feel equally and which will be apparent almost at once. If that is the case, exit as quickly but as gracefully as you can. An engagement with that person will never work!

Writing proposals (or letters of confirmation)

This may not occur until after your chemistry meeting. If that is the case, it is not, in my view, a proposal as such but simply a record for both parties of what has been agreed and in particular fees and timings.

If a prospective client asks for a written proposal before you have a chemistry meeting, it may indicate that either the value that you will deliver is unclear to the client (or not immediately relevant to them) or that they simply want something in writing that confirms your conversation and that can be used to gain agreement from colleagues or simply act as a record of what was discussed. It is obviously important to clarify what the client is seeking so that the document meets the correct need. The approach to structuring the document will differ accordingly.

If the aim is simply to confirm what has been agreed by way of next steps and fee arrangements, all that is normally required is an e-mail setting out the key items in bullet point form. As a rule that type of e-mail should cover:

- the key results to be delivered and how these are to be measured;
- the start date of the engagement and the duration or the number and approximate timing of sessions (eg six sessions of 60–90 minutes at approximately monthly intervals);
- the fee amount and payment basis (eg £5,000 + VAT with 50 per cent paid at the start of the engagement and the remainder at the end of the first quarter);
- the fact that what is said in sessions is confidential (unless there is a legal requirement to disclose);
- who is to be involved in any review process and when that review is to occur.

If you have terms and conditions covering things like cancellation or postponement of sessions, these should be attached and it is sensible to refer to them in the main body of the e-mail.

I have come across cases where the client's firm asks for a hard copy letter of confirmation with a 'wet' signature. However, that is increasingly rare and I have come across it only in the banking industry where the firm in question took the view that it was a compliance requirement of some kind.

In the event that the client asks for a more formal written proposal that can, for example, go to a senior colleague for sign-off, it will be necessary to cover the ground more fully. In effect this is a re-pitch for the business and you will need to replay the information you gathered in your initial meeting with the client, including the results you expect to deliver (ie the value to the client), the fee and the way in which you propose to handle the engagement. By reading the letter the person whose approval is needed should be able to follow the linear process of information gathering and value articulation almost as though they had been present in the initial meeting.

I recommend that this is done in the form of a letter rather than a basic e-mail – although the letter may in fact be sent as an attachment to an e-mail. The format of the letter is similar to that of a meeting planner. Following an introductory sentence along the lines of 'Thank you for your time; I enjoyed our conversation', the letter then sets out:

- The purpose of the letter (eg 'to confirm the points that we covered during our conversation').

- The results that you want to deliver for the client as a result of reading the letter (eg 'so that you and your colleagues can see the issues that we plan to address during this engagement, understand the outline engagement process and the benefits that will be delivered and confirm next steps').

- After that introductory paragraph, it outlines (in bullet point form) the issues identified by the client that frame the commercial fit (where you can make a significant difference to the client), where possible using the word choice of the client in the meeting.

- Next it sets out the issues that you will address and any that you cannot or will not.

- The heart of the letter is the benefits/results that you will deliver. I suggest that you insert a new section heading such as 'Benefits to you of this engagement'. Again this section can be in bullet point form, but I often find that it is more effective to use a series of short paragraphs.

- Finally you can outline the process of the engagement – ideally in a couple of sentences. This can include items such as feedback loops and confidentiality if appropriate.

- At this point, I suggest inserting a new section heading such as 'Fee arrangements'. I have seen the term 'Commercial aspects' used but prefer to avoid it. In that section, state the fees that you propose and the basis on which they are to be paid. I do not recommend any indication that they are open to negotiation; if the primary buyer wants to negotiate they will say so.

The whole letter can normally be constructed in two pages. I recommend that you limit it to three pages at most because of the 'too much information confuses...' phenomenon. Any details such as terms and conditions or a detailed description of process if required can be added as appendices.

Goal setting

Whether you use the 'GROW' model for coaching sessions or not, my experience indicates that goal setting is the most critical aspect not only of each session but of any coaching engagement as a whole. Clear and realistic goals tend to lead to good results.

It may be necessary to spend a considerable proportion of the initial session on gaining clarity of the client's goals and in challenging them to be more aspirational if appropriate. If there is a mismatch between the client's goals and those set by the primary buyer (in the case of business or executive coaching where the end client is not the primary buyer) it will be necessary to go through as many iterations as necessary to ensure that the two are aligned. Indeed that may become the primary focus of the initial session with a new client.

In some cases, the move towards more aspirational goals takes time so a review and possible expansion of goals becomes an important first step in each session. It is also important to make sure that the goals the client proposes are aligned with those set at the outset of the engagement. If not then it may be necessary to review the new ones with the primary buyer if that is not the client.

Obviously it is essential to ensure that goals are realistic if also aspirational. In some cases, it will become clear that the 'BiHAG' (Big, Hairy, Audacious Goals) so beloved of major management consultancies are not achievable by the individuals tasked with delivering the necessary outcomes; they simply do not have the required capabilities and/or the appetite for hard work. That can of course lead into a very different coaching conversation and perhaps a different engagement. It may also indicate that the engagement may be short-lived.

Changes in goals can indicate breakthroughs or blockages; sometimes even that the client is using the adjustment of goals as a form of displacement activity to avoid addressing fundamental issues. Either way it is important to look beyond the goal of the moment in order to keep the engagement on track.

Session duration and frequency

How long is 'a session'? The simple but somewhat unhelpful answer is 'It depends...'

Factors to consider include:

- complexity of the issues to be addressed;
- the attention span of the client and of the coach; and
- the time availability of both client and coach.

Complex issues will typically take longer to unravel, so a session of 90 minutes to two hours may be appropriate. If the attention span of either client or coach will not sustain that length of session it may be necessary to reduce the duration of each session but increase the frequency and number of sessions accordingly. That may affect the profitability of the engagement to you, depending on how you set your fees. Once you agree a fee for an engagement it will be hard to change it. This is one of the reasons why I prefer to agree a fee that can cover a period of engagement (eg six months) with (within reason) unlimited access by the client for support by phone or e-mail between sessions and which is still likely to be profitable for me. In other words the fee level has to be high enough for an increase in the number of sessions not to matter unduly, especially if some of them can be carried out by phone.

In terms of the availability of time (both for you and for the client), it may simply not be practicable for you to offer a client a series of two-hour sessions even if that would provide greatest impact for the client. Similarly, I have a number of clients who perceive themselves to be unduly busy, so that it is hard to get them to commit to sessions longer than 30–45 minutes in length. It is certainly possible to run effective sessions in that timeframe, although it requires laser-like focus on the part of both client and coach and often the use of a more directive approach to the coaching. In most cases, I find that the benefits of these short, 'micro-sessions' are sufficiently clear for the client quickly to become willing to commit more time. In some cases, they find the pace and results focus of these sessions stimulating and elect to run the whole engagement in that manner.

In other cases there may be a need to trade off shorter session duration against more frequent sessions. In other words, over a six-month period you may expect to spend say 15 hours with the client, face to face. In a 'standard' engagement that might equate to six or seven sessions each lasting around two hours, with an initial session of three hours. Alternatively you might find that the client is unable to work effectively with you for more than an hour to 75 minutes at a time. In my experience that is more likely if you elect to coach remotely (for example by telephone or video conference). In that case, you might find yourself delivering a dozen or more such sessions at two-weekly intervals. On the face of it, that is OK. However, you will need to factor in things such as travel time if the sessions are delivered face to face at the client's premises in order to ensure that the logistics and profitability work for you.

If possible it is worth having a conversation with the client about their preferences for meeting length and their 'meeting stamina' (attention span) before finalizing the fee arrangements. Once you have agreed to an engagement pattern and a fee at the start, it is quite likely that a change of pattern may prove to be necessary as you go along. In my experience it is hard to increase the fee, however.

Time-keeping in sessions

It seems to me that there is no single 'right' answer to time-keeping in sessions. There are several factors to balance:

- Your time is limited. If you use more time than planned in a given session, it cannot be recycled.

- A breakthrough may occur towards the end of a session, which can be capitalized upon only by extending the session beyond its planned end.

- Some clients may simply need to talk their way through a problem and a time boundary may impact their ability to attain a resolution.

- By the same token some clients may simply want to talk in order to avoid the need for commitment to action or indeed to take action.

In general terms it is good practice to keep within pre-agreed time boundaries. By doing so, you indicate respect for the client's time as well as your own. It is also possible to use the approaching end of a session as a way to encourage a positive decision or conclusion. By saying something like 'We have only ten minutes left of our allocated time. What decisions or next steps can we confirm at this point?' you draw attention to the need for decisions and can help the client to separate what is 'doable' at that time from what needs further discussion and why. In some sessions, it becomes clear that there is more to do. If both you and the client agree to extend the session by all means do so. I have seen some excellent breakthroughs as a result of an additional 20–30 minutes in a session. This is one area where intuition and common sense should override the mechanics of the clock.

Listening and the use of silence

'Active listening' is often named as the number one skill of an effective coach, yet it appears to mean somewhat different things to different people. I have previously mentioned the distinction between 'listening to understand' and 'listening to respond'. The latter is important in order to keep a conversation going. The former is vital in order to coach effectively. It also includes the whole gamut of responses: challenge, reflection, clarification, rephrasing etc. It is of course listening not only so that you yourself can understand but so that you can through your coaching enable the client better to understand what they themselves have said and to explore what is, as yet, unsaid.

When listening, you can of course choose your time to respond to what you hear. One of the most powerful weapons in the armoury of any coach is silence. If you are able to keep quiet when it seems that the client may have more to say, your silence will often trigger a deep response that can lead to a breakthrough moment. If silence seems inappropriate (or even simply scary either for you or for the client) you can use basic 'filler interrogatives' – the 'Uh huh...' or 'OK...' response – that can encourage the client to continue. Remember, your coaching is there to help the client to dig deeply inside their own mind in order to gain insight and reach conclusions that might not otherwise be possible for them to achieve.

With that in mind, it is usually better if you spend far less time talking in a session than the client does. Your role is to enable the client to talk and to hear what is implied as much as what is said explicitly.

Note taking

Some record of the points covered in a session is essential, not least for future review in preparing a post-engagement review with the primary buyer, if required. Note taking is the obvious way to achieve this.

However, I prefer not to take many notes during a session, because I find that the act of writing impacts my ability to listen accurately and deeply. It is a good example of the inability of the human brain to multi-task at more than a superficial level. However, because I focus on listening during the session, I find it fairly easy to write up notes afterwards. I do this as soon as practicable after the end of the session in order to minimize the inevitable memory failures that occur over time. In addition I use a pre-prepared template to help capture information in a structured manner. It is similar to my meeting planner in outline.

FIGURE 8.1   Note taking template for coaching sessions

Success factors for engagement	1 2			
How will success be measured?	1 2			
Issues to be considered	1 2			
Goal for session at start				
Goal for session in final form				
Blocking factors identified	1 2			
Current reality				
Opportunities/ Options reviewed	1 2 3			
Actions agreed	**Action**		**By whom?**	**By when?**
Date/time/ location for next session				

A copy of this can be downloaded at **www.successasacoach.com**.

I often find that it is helpful to carry a pre-printed hard copy of this template to each session so that I can write up the key points by hand. I can then either type up the notes and expand them if need be or (more commonly) scan the handwritten notes and save an electronic copy to my computer. In the early years of my business, I used to retain a hard copy file for each client and would put all my meeting notes into the file. That became onerous and a significant use of limited space in my office. By mid-2005, I therefore decided to archive the hard copy files and moved to electronic copies only. Clearly that imposes requirements for security of the data and for backup. An approach to both issues is outlined in Chapter 11.

Other approaches to note taking include the obvious notebook or pad and pen/pencil and some form of voice recording. I have not tried the latter as I feel it might be a distraction for the client. I also feel that a recording is not a particularly efficient way to access key points from a session (although it obviously allows detailed examination of not only what was actually said but other factors such as tone of voice).

Whilst a digital dictaphone is a cheap and effective way to capture information, a friend of mine uses a Livescribe pen, which allows him to take notes whilst the entire conversation is recorded on the in-built mini SD card. If he writes notes on the special Livescribe paper, he can simply tap the pen on the relevant section of the notes and the recording will play back from that point. Once again, I feel that this is not ideal as the fact of recording will likely distract the client and may give rise to fears over confidentiality, which would impact the willingness of the client to open up. It would, in many countries, be illegal to record a session without the knowledge of the client.

That said, I do in some cases use video during sessions with the deliberate aim of introducing an element of external stress, the level of which can be increased or reduced quite simply through the process of the session. The purpose is usually to allow the client to see themselves under differing levels of stress so that they can decide which of the somewhat differing personas they see as the most effective, and hence begin to understand and hence to control the perceptions they generate when communicating. The video camera is clearly visible but seems not to act as a distraction in the same way as a voice recording being made. I have no idea why this may be the case.

Action points/next steps

Agreeing concrete actions is probably second to the setting of clear goals as the most important success factor in a coaching session. If you end the session without next steps being agreed, it seems to me that what has occurred is a conversation rather than coaching. A conversational approach is all well and good, but coaching and conversation serve different purposes. The actions/next steps form the essential output from the session. They also act as part of the ongoing quality assurance of the engagement as a whole. If there are no meaningful actions/next steps it will be hard to prove the delivery of benefits if that ever becomes necessary.

Before ending a session, it is essential to agree what actions the client will take and by when. Clearly, the client must 'own' those actions and I find that the degree of felt ownership increases if the client is the person to write them down. If you have a flip chart in the room, it is an ideal way to capture what the client will do. If possible, the client should write the actions on the flip chart; that strengthens the psychological contract that they are making with themselves (and with you) to deliver the requisite results and to do so within a given timeframe. Where appropriate add a specific measure of success. This part of a session can become quite tense, especially if the session has involved challenge. The more challenging the session, the more important it is for the client to capture their own action points/next steps. If you do it for them, you own the actions not the client.

If there is no flip chart available I recommend asking the client to write down their actions/next steps independently and then read them back to you. You can take notes. However, the client should then be asked to type up the list of next steps and e-mail them to you, along with other key points from the session. That once again reinforces the psychological commitment that has been made. It may also highlight differences between what you have noted and what the client sends to you – which can form an interesting start to the next session. You might also consider asking the client to add to their notes/action points some feedback for you on what they thought went especially well during the session or where they felt a sense of breakthrough/insight and also what they felt could have been better for them or done differently.

Like goals, actions/next steps should conform to the old 'SMART' acronym: Specific, Measurable, Achievable, Realistic, Time limited. An action without a 'by when' date attached to it is no more than an aspiration. The last action/next step should be the date/time for your next contact with the client. That may be the next session but it may also be an interim phone call or e-mail exchange. The important thing is to get the date and time firm in both your diary and the client's.

The end of an engagement

All engagements come to an end. The way in which you end an engagement will determine the likelihood of being re-hired to do further work with that client or the client's firm and also the likelihood of the client providing good referrals for you. As discussed previously, these are the life-blood of your business. There are two aspects to be considered:

1 the final session with the client; and

2 any review with the primary buyer (if that is not the client themselves).

Prior to the final session with the client, you will need to review the success factors and measures that were agreed at the outset and assess realistically how well you and the client have done in achieving the aims you agreed at the start of the engagement. I recommend that you ask the client to do the same and to put down their answers in writing to you before the final session, along with any issues that remain outstanding plus (if possible) how they would like to address these. Many clients will find it helpful if you provide them with a short template such as the one shown in Figure 8.2.

FIGURE 8.2   Template for engagement review and client feedback

	Items to consider	On a scale of 1–10, how well did we do?	What went well? What could have been done differently or better?
Success factors for this engagement			
Measurement criteria			
What issues were addressed successfully?			
What issues remain outstanding?			
How effective did you find the process of coaching?			
Is there anyone else you know with whom you feel I could / should work?			

A copy can be downloaded at **www.successasacoach.com**.

The final session serves three purposes:

1 to cover off any outstanding issues for the client that form part of the engagement, ie this is a 'normal' session in its own right;

2 to review the engagement as a whole (a kind of quality assurance process) to ensure that the client has gained at least as much from it as expected; and

3 to allow you to explore further opportunities to work together and ask for referrals.

You will usually need to allow additional time over and above the norm for a session with the client in question in order to cover the review and referral process. The latter may require a further meeting if it becomes clear that there are indeed referral opportunities. That meeting will form part of your marketing activity rather than part of the engagement and its aim will be to qualify the referrals and ensure that you can be set up in the appropriate role in each case.

In an ideal world, the client will tell you that you have over-delivered against their initial expectations. Rather than allowing yourself to bask in that warm glow of success, it is important to clarify how the client has measured the benefits they have gained, ie to quantify the results. Many of the factors you will hear mentioned will in fact be 'soft' items such as 'improved internal relationships' or 'better relationships with customers' or even 'I just feel better with less stress'. It is important to ask how these items manifest in their day-to-day life at work and at home to see if your coaching can be linked to more concrete results whether in terms of the firm's bottom line or domestic happiness. The answers may become part of your marketing collateral by way of 'testimonials'.

In terms of referrals, this final session may be the last opportunity for you to ask this particular client for a referral, at least for some time. It is vital to seize it but equally vital not to be perceived as unduly aggressive. In a business context, a simple 'Is there anyone else in your firm or elsewhere that you feel I should meet?' may be enough. When the client is a private individual, a variation such as: 'Do you feel that any of your friends or acquaintances could use my help?' might be reasonable. The point is simply to ask a light-touch question that encourages the client to think about referring you on. In the vast majority of cases, the client will not do so unasked.

A review with the primary buyer ('PB') will follow a similar process, except that it should be done soon after your final session with the client for you to write up your session notes and prepare a briefing for the PB that includes:

- a statement of the aims and success factors agreed at the start of the engagement;
- a short review of what went on during your sessions such as the main points of difficulty/challenge and the actions agreed;
- the client's assessment of benefits delivered plus any concrete measures (if possible quote the client's words verbatim; it is far more powerful);
- your assessment of the success of the work and any recommendations for follow-up.

This document should not be longer than two pages and should be sent as a draft to the client for review before it is sent to the PB. In the (hopefully unlikely) event that the engagement has been less than wholly successful, it behoves you to be realistic and honest in your assessment. If possible, ask the client to send that document to the PB with a copy to you, stating that they have reviewed it and feel it is a sound report on the engagement and its outcomes. If the client wishes to add a positive endorsement, so much the better.

Obviously you cannot follow this latter approach if the relationship with the client is conflicted in some way. However, if that is the case, it should have been flagged to the PB at an early stage and the conflict resolved. The final review might need to be supplemented or replaced by a 1:1 meeting with the PB to talk about the conflict issues. If a conflict issues arises during an engagement and cannot be resolved it is usually best to end the engagement prematurely, even if that means forgoing fees or even refunding fees that have been paid up front.

Pulling the plug

No matter how well you set up each engagement there will come a time when things go wrong. There may be all kinds of reasons but in my experience, they tend to fall into one of four categories:

1 Forcing the fit at the outset (convincing yourself that there is a viable engagement where you can make a significant difference to the client when that is not in fact the case).

2 The aims of the PB and of the client differ and each seeks different outcomes from the engagement. This may not become apparent until after the engagement begins if there is a lack of trust between PB and client.

3 The client proves to be unwilling (or unable) to make the behavioural changes needed to deliver the results that have been agreed.

4 The client seeks to use the coaching engagement as a form of displacement activity to avoid taking action to address real issues or (rarely) uses the fact that they are being coached as a means to enhance their status with colleagues.

Each will require you, in the end, to terminate the engagement. However, the approach to termination will differ somewhat. Whatever the underlying cause of the problem, the sooner it is addressed the better and the less damage will be done to the relationship. If in doubt, openness and honesty will always serve you well.

In the first case (forcing the fit), a simple *mea culpa* is a good starting point. Explain why you felt that the engagement was viable and what has changed. It may be that the client or the PB can adjust the results they seek to make the engagement viable and allow you to re-start. If not, I would always offer to refund fees, wholly or in part. It is far better to make no money on an engagement than to leave a sour taste in the mouth of the client or PB. You will all have wasted time and effort and you may feel that you were misled into the engagement. That is immaterial; preserve your good name and your dignity and extricate yourself as painlessly as you can.

If the aims of the client and PB turn out to differ as you get into the engagement you have three courses of action open to you, and your chosen approach will depend on the nature and degree of the issue. You can:

- set up a meeting between PB and client to talk about the issue and resolve it or gain the agreement of the client that you may discuss and resolve the issue with the PB;

- adjust the engagement to fit the needs newly identified by the client but without reference to the PB; or

- terminate the engagement.

The first is obviously the least painful if it is practicable. It begs the question why the difference of aims occurred in the first place and that in turn may indicate wider organizational or inter-personal issues around which you will need to tread carefully. The second approach is fraught with danger but may be the only option in a situation where the client has been a victim of a problem such as bullying by the PB. That is the kind of situation that begs to be taken to supervision and in any event needs to be treated with extreme care. Whatever you do, ensure that your record-keeping around the engagement is flawless; if things go wrong you may need to be able to produce an auditable record of events.

Termination is of course a last resort but not one to be avoided at all costs. If the differences between client and PB are the tip of an iceberg of conflict – which is often the case – it may well be better for you to withdraw than to try to manage the problem. Once again, be prepared to forgo fees. It will be cheaper in the long run.

I find it not uncommon for clients to be unwilling to make changes to their behaviours or activities. In many cases they see the benefits but those benefits do not, ultimately, justify the perceived cost in terms of the work required. I have found that especially prevalent when working with senior individuals in professional services firms on issues around business development.

In some cases they find that they are moving out of their comfort zone when building their professional networks or having initial meetings with potential clients. For some, the adoption of a methodical approach such as I recommend appears to lack 'flair' and they pay lip service to it rather than practising it until it becomes routine and they see success. In some cases the engagement can be salvaged through some explicit challenging and perhaps an extension of the engagement reinforced by some robust leadership by the PB. In others termination is the only answer although that may in fact mean refusal to roll over or extend an engagement. Don't forget that you will be coaching for your own fulfilment as much as for the benefits you deliver to the client, the outcome of which is the income you receive.

If the client is using a coaching engagement as a smokescreen or as a status enhancement, it may be tempting to take the money and make an easy time of it. Whether you choose to do so is a matter for your own moral compass. I would find it hard to work with a client that was not genuinely seeking to improve their capabilities and would far rather look for another who did.

In any event, I recommend two things:

- Make sure that there is a termination clause in your terms and conditions.
- Make sure that you can clearly decide when to pull the plug on an engagement and invoke the termination clause. This can be linked all the way back to the factors that represent your 'perfect client', or rather to the reverse of those factors.

In the next chapter we turn to the structure of your coaching practice and the mechanics of making it work, before looking at strategic client leadership and your business systems.

CHAPTER SUMMARY

- Success in your coaching sessions can be defined as a combination of:
  - results for the client;
  - the degree to which your relationship with the client has been enhanced; and
  - the willingness of the client to provide referrals, to act as a reference for you and to re-engage with you when appropriate.

- The initial chemistry meeting is also an information-gathering meeting that allows you to confirm both the personal and commercial fits and to see how to articulate the value you bring to the client. It also sets up the context for the engagement assuming that it goes ahead as desired. It therefore needs to be planned and run as any other meeting with a view to getting the client to talk as early and as much as possible.

- Proposals or letters of confirmation should be as short as practicable with the benefits you deliver clearly and explicitly linked to the needs of the client and to your fees.

- Terms and conditions serve to set clear expectations. They should be written in plain language and be no longer than necessary. The key points of confidentiality, liability, payment terms and cancellation policy can be covered in a single side of paper.

- Success in setting clear and realistic goals drives success in the entire engagement.

- Adjust the session duration and frequency to suit the issues under consideration and the attention span of the client. Recognize that this may change during the engagement and that this may not reflect in your fees.

- Time keeping in sessions may need to flex depending on the timing of a breakthrough or the level of engagement of the client. Some therapists insist on a finite time per session. My experience is that to cut short a session when a breakthrough moment occurs at the planned end time is counterproductive.

- Note taking during the session is usually necessary. However, I prefer to minimize this and write up the session immediately afterwards using a standardized template. Some coaches use a dictaphone to record sessions, wholly or in part. I find this a distraction for me and for the client.

- No session should end without formally capturing 'next steps'. Ideally the client should do this and e-mail you their notes. Psychologically they therefore own the actions rather than you.

- At the planned end of an engagement it is important to carry out a review to ensure that the results achieved have been at least as great as expected. If possible turn positive feedback into referrals. Where feedback is less good than you hope, find out what went wrong, learn from the error (if any) and do all you can to remedy the problem.

- Recognize that some coaching relationships simply break down and that this may be through no fault of the coach.

- In some engagements it will prove necessary to 'pull the plug' and terminate an engagement early. Be clear in your own mind why you are doing this and tell the client as objectively and gently as possible without pulling punches. Offer to refund any fees that have not yet been spent.

- Make sure that your terms and conditions include an early termination clause.

Structuring your business

09

The mechanics of structuring your business and its underlying systems and processes may seem deeply unglamorous by comparison with the frisson of excitement (or of fear) that comes with contemplating winning new clients or carrying out high-impact coaching sessions. However, if the underlying structure of your business is flawed, it will make it far harder for you to do those more exciting things successfully and effectively; you will build friction into your business and that is never a good thing.

In this chapter we look in more detail at:

- the legal structure of your business;
- some of the possible business models you might consider;
- the nuts and bolts of your physical location versus your mailing address (including how to ensure that the phone is always answered during business hours);
- accreditation and certification; and
- the infrastructure of your business, including some fundamental issues around your IT platform.

Before we dive in, a health warning. I am based in the United Kingdom. The legal and tax situation in other countries differs; indeed the position may differ between states/provinces in countries such as the United States and Canada. I am neither an accountant nor a lawyer, so what you read in this book is not professional advice as such but based only on my own experience and my understanding of English law and practice. I accept no liability for it, nor for any actions that you take as a result of what you read here. If you have any doubt about the basis or implications of your decisions, you should take appropriate professional advice relevant to your own location.

The legal structure of your business

The choice of business structure has two sets of implications: legal/ fiscal and in terms of the perceptions of potential clients. There are broadly three approaches available:

- sole trader;
- limited company;
- partnership (which may itself be a limited liability partnership or non-limited liability).

A *sole trader* means exactly what it says: you trade under your own name or you use a 'trading name' but list yourself as the proprietor. For example, if your name is Susan Smith your business in sole trader form might be called Susan Smith. If you prefer to operate (ie to trade) under the name Clarity Coaching, it would be Clarity Coaching, proprietor Susan Smith. In the United States, the latter approach is known as a 'DBA' name ('Doing Business As'), so the business would be called Susan Smith DBA Clarity Coaching.

For many coaches this is a simple and relatively easy approach to starting a business and of course the legal structure that you choose has no effect on the quality of your coaching. However, if your target clients are in larger organizations, there may be a prejudice against dealing with sole traders, or at least an expectation that any 'supplier' will operate as a limited company or LLC.

From a tax standpoint, the business and you yourself are one and the same so you are effectively self-employed. Any income you generate will be taxed as your own, offset by any allowable expenses. From a legal point of view also you and the business are one and the same, so any liability incurred as a result of your business activity will rest with you. In other words, if a client decides that you have caused damage in some way to them personally or to their organization, they may take legal action against you personally. Any compensation or legal costs awarded in their favour will fall to you personally to meet. Your whole personal wealth might be at stake.

For these reasons, many coaches adopt a limited company structure ('limited' being an abbreviation of the term 'limited liability'). The benefit is that the company exists as an entity in its own right and is legally separate from you. If the company is sued successfully, its assets may be lost but your personal assets are not at risk; hence the term 'limited liability'. In the United Kingdom, the company is taxed separately from you yourself, based on its profits. (In the United States, as I understand it, a LLC is transparent for tax purposes so that the owner is deemed to have received the LLC's income directly as if it were their own). ·

You can be paid a salary or dividends or a combination of the two by your company and will technically be an employee of the company (as well as being its director). As a director of a company, you have all the responsibilities of directors set out in the Companies Act 2006, including the preparation and submission of annual accounts and returns to Companies House (which are usually outsourced to your accountant, who will often act as company secretary if you appoint one).

In the United Kingdom, it is relatively simple to set up a limited company. Information can be found at the Companies House website, **www.companieshouse.gov.uk**. Click the 'Start a Company' tab on the navigation bar. There are numerous 'formation agents' who will set up a company for you at minimal cost. The responsibilities of a directorship may seem onerous but can in reality be discharged fairly easily, especially if you outsource them to a suitably qualified accountant or other professional.

In the United States, there are different types of limited liability company. One of the most common is the Limited Liability Company or LLC, sometimes called a 'C' corporation. Alternatively, the Subchapter S Corporation, (which is a special form of corporation that allows the protection of limited liability but direct flow-through of profits and losses to a personal income tax calculation) may be preferable. The taxation of C and S companies differs and indeed can vary between states so you should seek suitable professional advice before deciding which route to follow in your own situation. There is an explanation of the differences between S and C corporations at the *Entrepreneur* magazine website: **www.entrepreneur.com/encyclopedia/term/82690.html.**

Partnerships can be tricky in several ways. Unless the partnership is structured as a Limited Liability Partnership ('LLP'), the liability issues are similar to those of a sole trader. Tax treatment of partnerships can be complex and is beyond the scope of this book. The greater issue, to my mind, however is the governance of the relationships between the partners.

Obviously one must be convinced that the relationship of goodwill and cooperation on which the partnership is formed is likely to continue indefinitely in order to agree to form a partnership in the first place. However, one should never act simply on the basis of a handshake agreement. It is vital that a well-drafted written agreement is put in place in order to document expectations for all parties. That should in my view be prepared by a lawyer and should include:

- loans or other payments into the business by each party;
- the basis on which both expenses and profits are to be split;
- payments (such as salaries) that are to be made to each party;
- the mechanism for taking decisions about the business (including how to resolve any deadlocked decision);
- the basis on which assets are to be split if and when the business comes to an end; and
- the basis on which the partnership may be terminated including how to handle relationships with clients.

Partnerships are a great example of the old saying that 'good fences make good neighbours'. It is far better to take time in structuring a partnership at the outset than to risk conflict later.

In my own business, I chose the limited company route because I felt that the benefit of limited liability far outweighed any administrative complexity and that it might be beneficial to keep the income generated by the business separate from my personal income. I also felt that most of my target clients would expect to deal with a limited company rather than with a private individual.

Insurances and consents

Insurance is a specialist field and once again it will behove you to take suitable professional advice. However, as a minimum, I recommend that you look into cover for:

- professional indemnity;
- employer's liability;
- public liability; and
- legal expenses (including cover for tax investigations).

In the United Kingdom, the insurance cover available as part of the Member Benefits package of the FSB is valuable and probably outweighs the cost of FSB membership. They also have an insurance advisory department that can help you decide on the best cover for your needs.

Professional indemnity covers you for issues such as damage to a client resulting from your advice. It is not cheap and can be hard to find as by no means all insurance companies provide it. Employer's liability cover is a legal requirement in the United Kingdom if you employ staff. Public liability is arguably not a requirement but the cost is relatively low and it could be valuable if you were in some way to cause damage or injury to a third party in the course of your business.

Legal expenses/tax investigation cover is in my view a no-brainer. The cost to fund the time of your own lawyer/accountant in handling an investigation by the Revenue can be prohibitive. If you were to try to handle such an investigation yourself the time commitment would be tremendous. FSB membership provides a good level of cover but it is worth checking that it is sufficient to meet your needs.

If you use your own vehicle in the course of business, you will need to check whether you need additional or different insurance cover: client visits as part of your business will almost certainly not be deemed 'social and domestic' use. Similarly, if you use a room in your home as your office, you should notify the insurance company that provides your buildings and contents insurances to ensure that you are adequately covered.

You should check that there are no restrictions on the use of your home or part of it as an office. Those may arise due to local government restrictions ('Zoning laws' in the United States) or due to other considerations. For example, if you rent your home, you may find that the lease prohibits running a business from the property. Similar conditions may be contained in the deeds to your property even if you own the freehold.

There may be tax issues as a result of running a business from your home, which might give rise to a Capital Gains Tax problem. That is not very likely but it is wise to check before you decide where to locate your new business.

Physical location versus postal address

We have touched on the perceptions generated by a postal address for your business that is clearly a private house versus one that is a credible 'business' address. In reality, unless you do a large part of your work remotely (by telephone/video conference etc) you will find yourself working most often at the premises of the client, or in some 'neutral' location, whether that may be a quiet coffee shop or a meeting room you have rented by the hour in a set of serviced offices. To base your actual office at your home is a great idea in order to minimize cost. However, there are other considerations, some of which we look at below.

To use a 'virtual' office where mail can be received and forwarded and a phone can be answered in the name of your business is all that you may need to overcome that perception issue and (in the eyes of the client) translate your business from being a home-based solo-preneur to being a 'real' business. A simple Google search for 'virtual office' plus the name of your town or city will likely throw up numerous results. The cost of a virtual office can vary from £30 to £100 ($50 to $150) or more per month depending on location and the level of service provided. To be a fully-fledged 'virtual office', the service you select should offer:

- a postal address that is credible as a location for your business;

- mail forwarding facilities (so that the virtual office provider sends on mail to your home or other chosen address); and

- a dedicated landline telephone number that is answered in the name of your business during normal business hours (and ideally offers out-of-hours callers the facility to leave a message).

It is fine for the person answering 'your' phone to say that you are currently unavailable but you will call back within a given time period, say 90 minutes. A business where the only phone number is identifiable as a mobile/cell phone number can cause alarm bells to ring for some clients.

If you are the kind of person that thrives on the company of others, you may want to think about taking some space in a building that houses other small firms so that you can develop 'coffee machine friendships' and some form of social interaction at work. In some cases you may find that your office neighbours can become great clients and sources of referrals. If you do decide to rent office space, make sure that you are not locked in to a lengthy lease period. If you sign up for a five-year lease, you are committing to make rental payments. Also consider the possible additional cost of business rates (property taxes in the United States) if that is payable over and above the cost of the rent itself. You may have to pay for utilities such as electricity and internet access on top of your rent. Some providers of serviced offices such as Regus will offer an all-inclusive cost.

We look at the physical set-up of your office later in this chapter.

Business models

Your choice of business model will influence, if not actually dictate, the way in which you position your business with potential clients. It may also reflect in the name of your business (for example, using the word 'Associates' or 'Partners' in the business name conveys the idea that more than one person is involved). If you decide to use a term such as 'Associates' as part of your business name, it is wise to ensure that you do have one or two that can be mentioned to a client and who would respond positively if they were to receive a phone call from the client to check on the reality of the business relationship between you. I highly recommend that you do not use the term 'Partner' unless your business is structured as a partnership; it can convey all kinds of misperceptions.

In some cases the type of client you choose might influence the choice of business model. In situations where you seek to work with senior people in large organizations, it may be easier to win business if you are able to offer a 'one stop' solution to the coaching needs of the whole client firm. That would probably mean being able to provide a number of different coaches each with somewhat different skills sets or areas of expertise in order to address different needs within the client firm. That in turn might indicate a partnership or associates model for your business. However, in my experience, this is relatively rare and most clients will be single individuals or small groups who will elect to work with you personally rather than with another coach of your choice from within your group. (Some clients might consider it a 'bait and switch' if you yourself win business with them but arrange for someone else to do the work.)

Five business approaches

There are five basic business models (as distinct from the legal structure of your business). I think of them in terms of film or book titles:

- The Lone Ranger;
- Batman and Robin;
- Brothers in Arms;
- Oliver Twist;
- Wall Street.

The *Lone Ranger* model is essentially what the name implies. You are the sole proprietor of the business and carry out all or most of the tasks involved in running it, including the majority of the administrative work. This is the way in which most coaches begin unless they decide that, based on their own psychological preferences, they need to work alongside others and so work as part of a partnership or corporate grouping. The Lone Ranger model has the virtue of simplicity and clear accountability for success. If you do not win the work and deliver it successfully, you eventually starve. Any income that is generated by the business is 'yours' to the extent it is not earmarked for items such as tax payments. However, it can be a hard existence for those who are not happy with their own company.

In many – perhaps in most – cases, the Lone Ranger develops into *Batman and Robin* through the process of outsourcing aspects of the business, leaving the owner to focus on winning work and delivering it with clients. In this case, the 'Robin' of support roles may be filled by one person or several and each may be 'virtual' (the 'virtual PA', the 'virtual finance manager' etc). Sometimes the Robin may be an associate used to fulfil a particular role with a certain type of client; for example a person who is a native speaker of some foreign language where that is required. Once again, this model is fairly simple because the ownership of the client relationship is clear and the support role is also clear and unambiguous.

In both the 'Lone Ranger' and 'Batman and Robin' business models, your ability to generate income is a function of the time you are able to spend on delivery with clients multiplied by the fee rate per unit of time or per session that you are able to charge. That applies regardless of how you set your fees and the basis on which you articulate your fee arrangements to clients. That is not to say that your income will be low; merely that it will ultimately be capped. It also means that your business is unlikely to have a value to anyone else; it is not saleable because the business is essentially you. As my wife puts it 'The clients rent the contents of your head'.

The *Brothers in Arms* approach is a catch-all to describe both the associates and the partnership business models. The legal structures of the businesses differ but many of the issues are similar. The key questions are:

- Who wins the business?
- Who owns the client relationship?
- Who gets paid what percentage of the net income?
- Who does what?

The first two items get to the heart of the matter. Without clients, there is no business. In my experience, it is rare for each person in a partnership or among a group of associates to have the same capability to win business or, having won it, to manage the client relationship effectively in order to maximize both retention and referrals. That is nothing to do with the ability of the individual to coach. It has everything to do with their sales and marketing skills and their willingness to apply and/or develop them.

In many cases, coaches who might otherwise have been successful Lone Rangers join a group of associates because they know that one or more of that group has good sales skills, which they feel to be lacking in themselves. They might therefore be able to reduce their sales effort in favour of coaching. In my experience, that inevitably introduces strains into the business relationship, which can be alleviated only by some differential split of net income. For example, the person who wins the business receives say 10 per cent or 20 per cent of the total fee for the engagement regardless of their delivery of coaching sessions.

As part of the Partnership (or Associates') Agreement, it is vital that the basis of the split of gross or net income is clearly defined. It is also vital to define roles and responsibilities within the business. It is perfectly viable for one person to do more of the sales and marketing activity if another takes on book-keeping and financial control. However, each party must agree that the effort involved in each role is adequately reflected in the income split.

Another reason for coaches to form groups of associates (and indeed partnerships) is the ability to have conversations about the business with others who are directly involved. That need not imply co-locating in the same physical office but probably will mean setting up regular routine meetings, either face to face or by conference call. Someone will need to assume responsibility for organizing and chairing such meetings and whatever technology you choose (if not face to face) must work flawlessly.

It is unwise to underestimate the impact of suddenly working solo if one has been used to a group environment. To join a group of associates can provide a valuable source of social interaction at work as well as (in some cases) enabling you to win clients with complex needs.

The *Oliver Twist* approach is where a coach agrees to 'go onto the books' of an organization that acts as a broker of coaching services and 'matches' coaches to specific client needs. That coach is effectively asking for work to be handed to them ('Please, Sir, can I have some more...?') in return for a (sometimes hefty) percentage of the fee for the engagement. If the coach has no desire to undertake their own sales and marketing activity but seeks only to coach, that approach is perfectly viable. However, it makes it harder for the coach to choose with whom they work, which in my view is one of the main benefits of running one's own business. It also places the volume of work that the coach undertakes under the control of a third party, something that many will be unwilling to do, certainly not to place all their eggs in that particular basket.

The *Wall Street* business model is essentially a corporate one where the business operates rather like one of the better-known consulting firms. That means that issues such as payment to individuals will have been resolved long ago as will issues of roles and responsibilities. It might therefore be an 'easier' transition for someone coming out of a prior corporate life into coaching. I know of only one such firm that has been successful (Praesta) and I am led to believe that they will not normally take on individuals who are not already experienced coaches with experience of running their own business. It is not the sort of approach that is likely to be available to the novice. This is perhaps the only type of business that has a life and hence a potential value beyond the involvement of the founders/owners.

However, this kind of business model has its own issues, not least the question of whether the individual coach wishes to operate in a corporate-type culture with a degree of management oversight. The compensating factor is of course that the firm of which one becomes a part can provide an infrastructure that is more robust, not to say luxurious than might be possible as a Lone Ranger. In joining such an organization, one is effectively becoming an employee (or at best a director) of the business with the attendant responsibilities and structures.

Choice of business model

In my experience, most coaches decide to operate initially as 'Lone Rangers' or in 'Batman and Robin' mode. This is a good way to explore the realities of running your own business and to test out your ideas on branding, positioning, target clients etc. The cost to run such a business can be minimal and you maximize your flexibility. Many 'Lone Rangers' develop into a 'Batman and Robin' model as they take on more work and/or it becomes more complex. They simply buy in support for coaching that falls outside their field and set in place an agreement that precludes the supporting coach from poaching the client. Clearly any such contract is worth no more than your ability to enforce it. Some aspects of the business can be outsourced but your own coaching cannot.

I have seen few partnership/associates models ('Brothers in Arms') work effectively long term, although they may be successful initially. The breakdown is usually driven by either failure to document the basics of income splits and roles/responsibilities at the outset or by the fact that one or other of the parties proves to be more successful in winning work than the rest. Large groups tend to sub-divide into duos or trios and these eventually sub-divide again. Some may re-form but many do not.

I am sceptical about the value of a broking model for the coaches involved, although it is clearly a good business for some of the brokers and can save the buyers of coaching a considerable amount of time in research and selection. It can also give both parties access to coaches/clients that might not otherwise be possible. The same is true to a degree of the 'corporate' ('Wall Street') model. However, as mentioned previously, successful coaching organizations of this type are few and far between.

As a rule of thumb, I have decided that I am willing to have employees (or rather contractors) in my business and to use associates selectively but not to take on partners. As someone who is (as a friend of mine describes it) essentially feral, I would not seek to join a corporate-type organization once more, having spent over 20 years working in large firms. However, I would not discourage anyone else from doing so if they like the corporate culture and benefits.

Recruiting partners or associates

If you decide that you prefer to work with others rather than solo and are willing to brave the issues that can arise in so doing. It may be that you seek partners or associates actively, or you may simply meet like-minded individuals with whom you feel it would be good to work. Before you embark on working with others, it is essential to decide (a) on what basis you wish to work together (associate or partnership); and (b) what factors will influence your selection of colleagues.

Rather than leaping straight into a partnership arrangement, I suggest that you test the waters by working with others as associates: it is far easier to terminate an associate arrangement that is not working satisfactorily than it might be as a partnership. Thinking about the factors that represent a 'good' associate for you is not unlike thinking about what factors define a 'perfect' client. The key is the values and behaviours rather than simply the skills set of the individual. In my experience, if you enjoy the company of the individual and find conversation with them easy, that is usually a good indicator that the relationship will work. The selection of people with whom to work is not trivial. In corporate life we do not usually have the opportunity to select our colleagues. In your own business it is a valuable blessing.

Accreditation and certification

We have touched on accreditation and certification in Chapter 1. However, this is for many coaches such a fundamental consideration that it is worth exploring in more detail here.

To be clear on terminology, training courses can be accredited; individual coaches can be certified. The basis of certification will usually include a stipulation that the individual has successfully completed an accredited training course. It will also often be necessary to have an amount of documented experience in coaching in order to gain full certification, including some client references. There may also be a requirement for ongoing supervision and/or CPD.

The mere fact of completing an accredited training course in coaching does not, of itself, mean that you are an effective coach, nor does it mean that you will be successful in winning clients. However, as mentioned in Chapter 1, completion of an accredited course is becoming more important for some clients as a selection criterion for coaches. The same is true of certification. To undertake an accredited training course may also be valuable in terms of your own self-confidence to offer yourself to potential clients as a coach. It avoids any issues of uncertainty in your own mind about whether you can in fact do the job effectively (or might help you to understand that you cannot...).

I have not been asked about my training or certification in a dozen years of running my own business and so far as I know have never lost a potential client as a result. Certification is not cheap either in cash terms or the time needed for record-keeping and undertaking the periodic re-certification process. That does not necessarily mean that you should take the same view; simply that it is a decision to be taken with due care. The position is undoubtedly changing, although the pace of change seems to me to be glacial at present and likely to remain so unless coaching becomes regulated in a similar manner to other professions such as the law and medicine.

The infrastructure of your business

Having decided on the legal structure of your business, you will need to deal with the minutiae of setting up its infrastructure. That is essentially:

- business bank account (and credit card processing if appropriate);
- tax arrangements;
- IT systems; and
- physical office space.

Bank account

Even if you will operate as a sole trader, it is good practice to have a separate bank account that is used for your business activities. That makes it far easier to keep track of both income and expenditure for the business and hence to prepare tax returns etc. In many cases it need be no more than a 'No 2' account in your own name with your current bank if you are a sole trader. If you are using a limited liability company or partnership structure, a dedicated bank account is a necessity.

It is worth shopping around for the best terms in selecting your business banking provider. Business bank accounts are rarely free of charge, beyond a small number of transactions per month, and the transaction costs can mount up rapidly. The FSB has a relationship with The Co-operative Bank, which does (at the time of writing) offer free banking for members and many other UK high street banks will offer free banking for a period, after which charges kick in.

If you work with clients in other countries you may need to have an account in each of the relevant currencies. Foreign currency accounts are often costly for you to operate so only go down this route if there is a genuine need to do so.

Think carefully about who is authorized to make payments out of your bank account and make sure that you keep a good eye on cash-flows into and out of the business. Regular checking of the bank account is the most effective way to monitor payment of invoices and prompt payment is critical to any business regardless of size.

You will certainly need either a debit or credit card associated with your bank account that allows you to make routine payments for items such as stationery, travel costs or buying the occasional lunch for a client. Some banks may be unwilling to issue a credit card immediately on a new business account. An alternative could be a provider such as American Express (Amex) who will charge you an annual fee for the provision of the card. However, in my experience Amex is not accepted by all retailers.

Depending on the nature of your clients, it may be necessary for you to accept credit and debit card payments for your services. The cost to have a 'merchant account' that provides you with the necessary facilities can be significant, even in terms of a monthly fee let alone transaction charges. If your bank is unable to provide a merchant account or the costs seem too high for you, an alternative might be PayPal which allows you to accept and to process payments online. In the event that you sell products such as reports, DVDs etc online via your website PayPal might be the only option at least initially. Depending on the particular PayPal account you select, there may be no initial set-up fee but each transaction will result in a fee of approximately 2–3 per cent of the transaction value. (See **www.paypal.com** for more details.)

Tax arrangements

From a UK perspective, the main issue is whether or not you need to register for VAT (Value Added Tax – or sales tax in the United States). The threshold for turnover above which registration for VAT becomes compulsory is currently over £70,000 per annum; well above the level that makes this relevant for many coaches. One can register voluntarily for VAT at any level of turnover. However, in terms of client perceptions, a non-VAT registered business may be seen by some to be unsuccessful and hence in some way 'less good' than one that is VAT registered. VAT registration does impose some additional book-keeping and administrative chores. However, it can allow you to reclaim VAT on items such as purchase of your computer, which may be significant.

You should seek professional advice on tax arrangements and the basis of calculation for tax liabilities. I outsource all tax and accounting arrangements to my accountants (**www.c-c-b.co.uk**). Unless you have a real desire to follow a DIY approach and the requisite knowledge, I suggest you outsource also. A good accountant with whom you can establish a good working relationship is an essential; a good lawyer is desirable.

It goes without saying that taxes must be paid in full and on time as and when they fall due.

IT systems

This sounds rather grand for what may be a one-person business. However, with modern technology you can achieve equal levels of effectiveness and robustness as a far larger corporation but at quite low cost.

We have already looked at some of the IT basics for your business back in Chapter 3. By way of a recap, basic requirements are a computer, an external hard drive (for backup), a printer and internet access, plus relevant office software. Whether you choose a PC or Mac is essentially a matter of personal choice. I have stuck with a PC on grounds of familiarity and cost, although I own an iPad. It is possible to buy a perfectly adequate laptop PC for less than £450. An equivalent Mac would cost roughly double that amount. An outline specification for a basic computer suitable for a 'Lone Ranger' can be found at **www.successasacoach.com**.

Some sort of *backup device* is essential. The probability that you will suffer a failure of the hard drive in your computer at some point is very high; indeed you should absolutely plan on it. Without a backup of your data you will be in deep trouble. It is possible to back up only your data files (such as documents, spreadsheets, etc) onto a suitably large capacity USB memory stick. However, in order to make a complete copy of your hard disk you will need an external drive that is of similar capacity to that in the computer itself. I use Acronis True Image software to create a mirror image of my laptop hard disk on at least a weekly basis. In fact I keep two different backups; one at home and one at my office in case one is stolen or destroyed by fire, as well as an online ('cloud') backup that runs automatically whenever the laptop is connected to the internet.

Online backup services such as Carbonite (**www.carbonite.com**) are very effective and ensure that you lose no data. However, to carry out a full recovery from your online backup is time consuming as the speed of recovery is limited by the capacity of your internet connection. If you have the data on an external hard drive, recovery is as rapid as the transfer of data from one drive to another. What might take several days via an online service takes an hour or so of transfer between disks. A note outlining the process for creating backups and recovering data using Acronis can be found at **www.successasacoach.com**. That note also covers in outline the use of other forms of backup such as a network attached storage (NAS) drive, dedicated server etc.

The cost differential (both to buy and to run) between laser and inkjet *printers* has reduced greatly over the last few years. However, a colour laser printer will still be somewhat more costly than an inkjet to buy although slightly cheaper to run. If you are likely to print photographs, an inkjet will be a better bet. Given the low cost differential, I would opt for an 'all in one' printer that can scan documents, be used as a photocopier and even act as a fax machine. Running costs will not usually be a major issue as the volume of material that you will print is likely to be fairly small. *PC Pro* magazine offers very sound reviews of hardware and software, including printers. Simply Google 'PC Pro reviews' to locate current recommendations.

Internet access is essential although speed is not likely to be a huge issue. Mobile internet access is now more common and many clients will expect you to be able to access e-mail whilst out of the office. That implies a need for some form of smartphone (or for a highly portable laptop or tablet with a mobile internet connection), although once again a fairly basic model is perfectly adequate.

For *office software*, the default choice for most clients will be MS Office. You therefore need to use MS Office yourself or use software that can open documents etc created in MS Office and save documents in a format that can be opened by an MS Office user. The most commonly used alternative to MS Office is Office Libre, which can be downloaded free of charge. It offers functionality that is broadly similar to the Microsoft version. Saving documents etc in the relevant MS format needs to be done manually; a small price to pay. Office Libre was formerly known as Open Office. However this was taken over by Oracle some time ago and many of the developers involved created Office Libre to offer a truly open source alternative. Some feel that it is now a preferable solution.

In looking at the need for your own website, we touched on the need to have a 'real business' e-mail address as opposed to one from a generic e-mail provider such as Hotmail or Google Mail.

Physical office space

You will need some kind of work space, whether at home or elsewhere. Don't forget that you will be spending only a relatively small proportion of your time actually coaching clients, especially in the early days, so you need a place in which to work on all the other aspects of your business. It need not be large and indeed it need not be a dedicated space, although it is exceedingly convenient if it is possible to close the door when you are working in order to avoid disturbance of – or by – any other family members etc. That door will also form a physical (and hence mental) separation between work and home.

For some time after starting my own business I lived alone and found that I could get by working at my dining table. I eventually found that it was inconvenient to clear the table of computer, papers etc every time I wanted to eat so graduated to a separate desk and a proper office chair. Even that began to get old after a fairly short time. I now have what is called (affectionately) the 'Super Shed' in the garden at home. It is only eight feet square inside but provides all the space I need. It has the advantage of being a 15-metre commute from the back door, which is enough to create a mental separation between home and work whilst minimizing the time needed to get to and from work.

The most important item of furniture in your office is your chair. It is perfectly possible to use any old dining chair or whatever you have to hand. However, you will quickly find that a chair that is simply not intended for office use will cause you discomfort, which may eventually result in muscular tension and even injury. A good office chair should be adjustable to suit your size and build (height of seat and back, tilt of both back and seat and height of any arm rests). There is nothing wrong in buying a second hand chair, if it is in good condition and made by a reputable firm. Even so, a decent chair will likely cost £200 plus. It is worth every penny in my view.

I try to minimize the amount of 'stuff' that I bring into my office and to reduce the volume of hard copy filing by scanning any documents that I need to retain where possible. The smaller the space you have available, the more ruthless you will need to be on tidiness and minimizing clutter. It is helpful to have your computer, your phone and your printer within reach simply by swivelling your chair. The fact that you do not have to get up from your chair to answer the phone or collect a sheet from the printer does increase your efficiency to a surprising degree.

Time allocation

Time is one of the most important elements of your business infrastructure. It is the only asset you have in running your own coaching business (even if you manage to avoid selling time to clients in favour of selling results). It is vital to use time effectively, which means allocating it specifically rather than simply using it ad lib and allowing work to expand to fill the available time. Effective time allocation requires:

- prioritization (so that you focus on what is important, not simply what is urgent);
- willingness to accept a sound 'fit for purpose' solution that can be delivered in a timely manner rather than seeking perfection;
- a realistic understanding of how much time you need to achieve that sound solution for each task you undertake;
- a commitment to yourself to spend no longer on that task than you have allocated;
- planning followed by implementation of your plan;
- avoidance of distractions whatever they may be; and
- building a system that works for you for each aspect of your business.

With that last point in mind, the final chapter focuses on building your business around good systems, including a method for task prioritization and time allocation that seems to work well in the real world. The next chapter explores the concept of strategic client leadership.

CHAPTER SUMMARY

- The legal structure you choose for your business will tend to set expectations in the minds of potential clients about the way you work and possible 'fit'.

- The legal structure and the operating model you choose need not be linked.

- Consider the respective benefits of being a sole trader, a limited company/LLC or a partnership. Each has different tax and liability issues. Take appropriate advice before deciding.

- Insurance is an essential item; don't be tempted to skimp on it. The FSB in the United Kingdom offers some cover as part of the membership package and has an insurance advisory department – among other benefits.

- Consider the relative merits in terms of cost and client perceptions of a virtual office address versus working from home and being seen to do so. It matters to some clients, not to others.

- If you plan to involve others in your business as Associates or Partners a written agreement setting out who does what, client ownership and percentage of fee splits plus the mechanism for winding up the business as and when necessary is vital.

- When recruiting partners or associates, the approach is similar to defining the 'perfect' client: values and behaviours trump pretty much all other considerations. If in any doubt about those factors, don't go ahead.

- To have completed an accredited training course as a coach is increasingly a requirement. Individual certification is for the time being less essential in my experience. However, that may well be changing.

- It is worth spending some time at the outset on the basic infrastructure of your business; a designated bank account, a 'professional' e-mail address based on your own domain name, etc.

- Even if you work at home, it is highly desirable to have a dedicated 'office' space, and ideally one on which you can shut the door. The most critical item of office furniture is your office chair and it is worth spending money on a good one, even if it is used.

- Your IT infrastructure must include effective data backup and security. By all mean include a 'cloud' solution but in my view do not rely on it as the sole backup.

- Time allocation is a critical element of your business systems; you cannot manage time, only allocate it. Find a downloadable report on the subject at **www.successasacoach.com**.

Strategic client leadership

10

An American friend of mine described the concept of strategic client leadership (SCL) as follows:

> Among your clients, you find a few great people where you see huge potential. You work with those few great people for a long time, helping them to see that they can achieve more than they ever thought possible and then enabling them to do it. By and by they become friends as much as clients. One day you find that your friends run these great companies and businesses and they know that they couldn't have done it without you.

SCL is a variation on the concept much discussed in business schools and in sales training courses of strategic account management (SAM). It differs in that SCL is applicable at a smaller scale of operation and at the individual client level, whilst SAM tends to be focused on managing a complex relationship at the organizational level. Although used mainly in the context of business coaching or executive coaching, SCL can in theory be applied to any client that is truly of strategic importance for your business, regardless of the field of coaching in which you operate. Clearly, you will need to determine what 'of truly strategic importance' means for you and for your business.

SCL is a fundamentally different approach from SAM, focusing on the way in which you can lead a given client (and through them their firm or organization) to understand their potential as you see it and, working with you, to realize that potential. (We have previously looked at this as 'commercial fit'.) A key factor is that you see potential and opportunities that the client does not – as yet. In that sense it is the ultimate business partnership model and can lead to a series of connected engagements, each building on the last over a period of time. It can be used in larger and more complex organizations although the initial focus is on one person: your selected client.

By comparison, SAM as conventionally practiced is more about how you manage the total relationship between your firm and that of the client; it is about process and control rather than partnership and it tends to be applicable where your firm involves several and distinct areas of work if not numerous people, and the client firm is large and its organization complex. It allows you to deliver the whole of your firm's capabilities (which may involve numerous people) to the client firm in order to maximize benefit for both parties.

Why can SCL be important for your business?

- It helps you to identify those clients where the long-term commercial fit is excellent (ie where you can continue to make a significant and growing difference to the client over a period of time, perhaps several years rather than a few months).

- You therefore (in theory at least) reduce the need constantly to win new clients (however it is essential to avoid complacency as we discuss later).

- You should be able to generate long-term income from the client firm if not from the individual client – based on the value that you deliver and the developing needs of the client.

- It takes the relationship to a deeper level where you (a) become recognized by the client as a critical component of their own success and that of their firm; and (b) you and the client develop a strong partnership that locks out your competitors (if any) and broadens the field of cooperation for you both.

- It helps you to focus your efforts on the clients where they are of greatest benefit so that you save time and effort and (potentially) increase your fee rate, not only for your SCL client(s) but across your business.

Not all clients qualify for treatment as 'strategic'. In most cases, you will simply undertake an engagement and at the end of the agreed period or number of sessions (whatever the engagement pattern may be) you review progress and draw the engagement to a close. If you are doing a good job of developing your business you will no doubt ask for referrals and follow up on those. You may keep in touch with a past client for a period of time but in many cases the engagement will be a one-off because part of the success of coaching is to achieve a long-term change that allows the client to make some kind of breakthrough. It is part of the job of the coach to – in effect – work themselves out of a job.

The idea of strategic relationships and of SCL comes into play where you are able to spot a longer term development opportunity, whether that is simply for the individual or for the firm that employs the individual or (ideally) both. You are looking to identify, among clients within your particular niche or field of activity, those individuals and firms that are likely to be the winners of tomorrow (even if they may not be one of today's high profile firms or individuals in their field). Ideally you should be able to see not only an immediate fit to work together but a series of opportunities that may come to fruition over time and perhaps only on the back of work that you undertake now. The 'strategic' element cuts two ways:

- the client (and their organization if relevant) can be of strategic importance to your business (for example a well-known company that would look impressive on your client list); and

- you can deliver value to the client at a strategic level, long term.

It is a mistake to push a client towards a SCL relationship unless you are convinced that the client both warrants it and is willing and able to make full use of it. Otherwise you risk setting inappropriate levels of expectation and consequent disappointment if these are not met. A step-by-step approach is usually possible, however.

It is hard to define exactly what marks out the type of individual that might warrant a SCL approach and indeed they can be found in any type of firm or field of work. In my view it is the individual that should be the focus of attention rather than their firm; really 'good' people are quite rare and, if they work for organizations, will typically do well within them wherever they go. They will often have an ability to do well in a variety of different fields. If your relationship is good and has been developed strategically there is a good chance that such excellent individuals will seek to bring you with them when they move into a new role.

I have been fortunate to work with a number of such individuals and although their fields of work differed and the nature of my work with each of them varied quite widely, there were some factors that I found to be common to all of them:

- a desire to do well in all aspects of their lives, recognizing that work was only a part of that whole;

- innate intelligence (not necessarily marked by academic qualifications), combined with constant intellectual curiosity, learning and personal development (one could call this quality 'native wit' or 'street smart');

- a strong work ethic and willingness to do the work needed to become expert in a given field;

- willingness to do less pleasant or less interesting tasks well; in other words everything they undertook was done to the same high standard;

- self-control, including knowing when and how to say 'no';

- realism and intellectual honesty without arrogance; and

- ability to communicate effectively and to build good personal relationships.

I have found those characteristics in people with widely differing backgrounds; from a Cambridge bio-chemistry graduate turned lawyer, to a young graphic designer producing hand-made T-shirts, to a graffiti artist turned designer and maker of stained glass windows, to a city operations and IT director transitioning into coaching. In each case, however, it became clear very quickly that each would be successful in their chosen field and that there would be (different and changing) opportunities for me to help them to achieve and to leverage that success. They would be winners over the long term and, in helping them, so would I.

SCL is not for everyone...

Embarking on a SCL relationship is not trivial; it will likely involve a lot of effort on your part over and above what you may consider to be a typical coaching engagement. You may not be paid by way of cash for all of it – and probably not in the early stages – although you will almost certainly reap huge rewards in terms of personal fulfilment. (If that is not one of the reasons for becoming a coach and your entire focus is on the income you can generate I wonder if you may be working in the wrong field...)

The point is that, not only are individuals that can benefit from a full-blown SCL relationship quite rare, the intensity of such a relationship is such that you can and should probably attempt to handle only a limited number at any given time. It is unwise to think of any 'good' client as one that should be treated 'strategically'. Good clients can offer many opportunities for you to help them. Some will be happy to have your help over long periods of time rather than for discrete and time-limited engagements. That does not make them strategically important for your business or candidates for a SCL approach.

What does the term 'strategically important' mean in this context? It may appear that to gain work with somebody employed by a big-name firm is of strategic importance for your business and indeed that may be so to the extent that the mention on your website of a 'Big Four' accountancy firm (for example) as a client can be attractive to some of your potential clients. However, in this case, I use the term to indicate the likelihood of:

- a long-term relationship with a client that has high potential, where

- you can see an excellent commercial fit beyond the current engagement that

- may not be apparent to the client but will allow them to achieve great success and where

- you can be a key enabler of the client's success.

My experience indicates that most coaches will come across relatively few such relationships.

Leaving aside the time and effort needed to make a success of a SCL approach with a given client, it is likely that the work with the client will extend beyond a conventional coaching approach into mentoring/consultancy. You will need to ensure that you are comfortable in doing so as well as ensuring that the client understands the changing nature of your role with them. (This will obviously form part of the contracting and goal-setting in the new relationship.)

If you elect to move to a SCL approach with a given client, it will, I believe, be necessary to set up a new engagement with them; in effect a re-pitch. The process of doing this is outlined below. It should not be undertaken lightly.

The relationship factor

Apart from a long-term commercial fit with several opportunities for you to enable outstanding success for the client, another key factor in deciding to upgrade from a normal coaching engagement to a SCL approach is the relationship factor. This has three aspects:

1 To what extent did you immediately 'like and trust' this person and recognize them as a potential star?

2 Where do you (realistically) think that your relationship with that person is today and to what level could it be developed?

3 In what role do you feel the client positions you in their own mind and how does this differ from the role that you would ideally seek with that person?

We have explored the importance of the immediate 'like and trust' factor as a precursor to doing business and some of the factors that underlie those positive perceptions. In this case the question is reversed; not what does the client feel about you but what did you feel about the client on first meeting and, having come to know this person better through a coaching engagement, how have your perceptions developed?

Separately it will be necessary to have an idea of how you would like to be recognized by the client in question; how you seek to position your role with the individual and with the firm (if they are not one and the same). A useful way to help you to articulate that role is to decide how you would like the client to complete the sentence 'I recognize [your name] as the person who...'

At this point we can look at where the relationship sits on an objective basis. I use the 'relationship pyramid' as a tool to consider the nature of client relationships. It is not dissimilar to the 2 × 2 matrix we used to consider the different types of buying decision in Chapter 5. We looked at the relationship pyramid in Chapter 7 in the context of fee setting and the potential elasticity of your fees. In this chapter we use the same tool for a somewhat different purpose and we add one more level: that of the true business partner and friend.

To recap, transactional relationships are driven largely by cost/benefit considerations and you will face competition on price and delivery. Like and trust are of some importance but not a deciding factor unless those perceptions are negative. A commercial relationship is akin to the choices you might make in selecting a builder to construct an extension to your home. Although price is a factor, you may not choose the cheapest quote and the 'like and trust' factor comes into play. The relationship will tend to be a one-off engagement although you may gain referrals or re-engagement if you maintain contact effectively.

FIGURE 10.1   Relationship pyramid 2

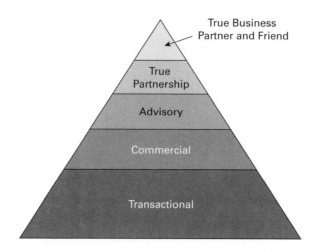

An advisory relationship is the main aim of many (perhaps most) people in the professional services field. They seek to be the preferred supplier to that client in a specific field or niche. Price is now less of an issue and, unless the role that the client needs to be filled changes, it is likely that you will continue to win work from that client for an extended period of time. The problem is that the relationship is limited to the given niche or field of work and has a ceiling (determined by your capability) above which the client may well look for alternative providers.

In other words, the role that you seek with that client needs to develop at the same, or greater, pace and in the same direction as the client's needs. If it does not, you will be supplanted by someone else who has positioned themselves to address the client's 'felt pain' in a different way and at a higher level. If you want to work with a given client on a long-term basis, you will need, therefore, constantly to reinforce and build on the relationship you have. Complacency will eventually bring the relationship to an end or limit it, perhaps significantly. To be in an advisory relationship is a good position but not necessarily a great position.

What marks out an advisory relationship? The nature of the conversation moves from mostly tactical issues ('How can I get ABC done...?') to more strategic ones ('What should I be doing about...?' or 'What could I do in order to achieve XYZ...?'). You will likely receive calls from the client outside the normal pattern of an engagement. You will begin to receive social invitations, although these may be in a business context (corporate entertainment-type events etc). You begin to know the client personally, to hear about family events and interests/hobbies.

A partnership-type relationship is stronger than an advisory one. Price becomes far less of an issue and the breadth of your involvement can increase; indeed it probably must increase if you are not to suffer from the eventual limitations of an advisory relationship. If you were a lawyer, for example, specializing in property/real estate work, you would need to consider broadening the relationship to include other aspects of the client's business such as employment law, acquisitions etc. That might well involve bringing in a colleague. In a coaching context, if you have achieved an advisory relationship you will need to decide whether you want to upgrade it and what would allow you to do so. In terms of the structure of your engagements with the client, you will find yourself doing work with them outside the formal structure of sessions. That may well change the way in which you wish to structure the engagement in the future; perhaps moving to a retainer fee basis rather than per session or per hour.

In a partnership relationship, the conversation with the client is likely to be largely strategic, big picture topics. The nature of your role changes, perhaps slowly and imperceptibly at first but you will find yourself engaged in conversation with the client more frequently outside routine sessions. At this point, therefore, you will almost certainly want to consider the structure of the engagement with the client if you have not already done so and it is quite likely that you will want to move to a retainer fee with this client. However, if you find opportunities to work with others in the same client firm, you may well wish to adopt a more structured approach with a set number of sessions for example in the first instance.

When you are in a partnership relationship with a client, the nature of the conversation is not only strategic, but also more personal. You may find yourself asked to discuss relationships with colleagues, key client relationships, family issues etc. For example, I found myself on one occasion discussing with a client the career impact of her unplanned pregnancy. Another client told me that I was 'the only person I can trust to tell me who's lying to me and why'. You will meet socially, outside any corporate entertaining events (although you may well be invited to those also). The client will no doubt expect that the social engagements will work two-way.

At the level of a true business partner and friend, you will be recognized by the client as in effect a member of the leadership team of their business, but who happens not to be directly employed within it full time. The nature of the conversation becomes strategic in the extreme although you will from time to time dive into knotty tactical issues. It will be robust and occasionally 'no holds barred'; indeed it may need to be in order that you can help the client to the best of your ability.

At this point, the price for your services becomes a minimal factor in the decision to retain you; the issue is only that you continue to deliver excellent value. Once again, your ability to deliver must match or exceed the needs of the client. Otherwise, over time your position as a true business partner will be eroded. You may well then retain a social involvement with the client but you will no longer be their 'go to' person. This is a dynamic relationship therefore, which will change over time and is not guaranteed to last or to remain at its peak. Unless you take action to maintain it, it will undoubtedly not do so. This is a level of relationship that requires more effort than most.

Where are you on the pyramid?

In considering whether you can or wish to elevate a particular client to a SCL approach in your business, the starting point is, based on the above, where does your relationship sit at present within that pyramid? The second question is where could it sit and what would be needed to take it to that level? Lastly, a critical question is, if you could take the relationship to a true business partnership, do you want to do so? (In other words, do you wish to make a long-term commitment to working with this client?) Your assessments must be brutally honest if you are to avoid wasting considerable time and effort.

As a reality check, for practical purposes, all client relationships will start at the transactional or commercial level. Many will remain there. That will become apparent either because you have no particular desire to commit to a re-engagement with the client once the first has drawn to an end, or, by the same token, that the client may not wish to continue.

In my experience, if you are able to re-engage with 50 per cent of all clients with whom you work, that is not a bad hit rate. Where you do re-engage, it is likely that you can achieve an advisory relationship with somewhere between 40 per cent and 60 per cent of those clients. Of those clients, you may move to a partnership relationship with up to 20 per cent and of that 20 per cent you may achieve a true business partnership with a further 20 per cent. Out of 100 clients therefore, you might re-engage with 50. Of those, you might reasonably expect to achieve an advisory relationship with say 20–30. Out of those advisory relationships you might achieve four to six partnerships and two of those might become a true business partnership.

Going all the way back to the definition of our 'perfect client' and the way in which you qualify clients at the outset, it is obvious that the more effective your qualification process, the higher your likely hit rate in gaining deeper relationships with clients, so that you can improve on the above rule of thumb figures.

In terms of timeframes, I believe that it would be hard to achieve a true business partnership in much less than 18 months. A decent advisory relationship might be achieved in six months or so. It will probably be hard to move towards a SCL approach until your relationship is realistically at the advisory level.

How to move to SCL?

Clients that merit a SCL approach should, almost by definition be capable of becoming 'true business partners' – right at the top of the pyramid. In the early stages of an initial coaching engagement, you will need to identify or confirm in your own mind:

- that this person has the hallmarks of a future star – ie most of the characteristics outlined above;
- that there is a real opportunity for this person to achieve exponential success – with your help;
- the potential end game – ie the aspiration (or simply what you can help this person to achieve);
- that this aspiration is one about which this person is passionate (or can become so once they understand the opportunity and give themselves permission to go after it);
- (in outline) the steps that would be necessary in order that this person can achieve the end state that you envision;
- that you yourself want to upgrade the relationship to a SCL approach leading to a true business partnership and why.

At an appropriate moment in the initial engagement, you will need to articulate the opportunity that you envision, the consequent benefits to the client and the results that they might reasonably expect to achieve. This will need to be done in terms that resonate with that person, having in mind the data gathered at the start of the relationship (even in your initial meeting) about what drives this person at an emotional level, their learning preference, how they take decisions etc. It is in effect a new sale that places you in a somewhat different role with the client; perhaps more akin to that of mentor rather than coach. Clearly you need to be comfortable with that change and how to manage the current engagement in a manner that is authentic whilst reinforcing the new role for the future and setting up a new engagement.

At this early stage, the articulation of the opportunity you see should be light-touch. It is quite possible that the client will not have seen this for themselves and it may appear 'just too big' for them at this point. Your coaching and leadership in that case will entail enabling them to give themselves permission to contemplate it, to understand that they can achieve that level of success and that they can co-develop with you a plan to overcome any intermediate hurdles. The client also needs to believe that you can enable them and are willing to support them in achieving the aim you outline. This will be a big commitment for both of you in terms of time and effort.

I do not recommend that you have this conversation about change of your role and nature of the future engagement during a coaching session. It would probably cause confusion in the mind of the client. I recommend that you tell the client that you have some ideas that you would like to discuss informally outside a session and ask for a short meeting (say 30 minutes) to do so. If possible, that meeting should probably be on neutral ground, perhaps over lunch or coffee at a local restaurant or café. The location needs to be quiet and reasonably private.

As ever, you will need to plan the meeting (use the Planner). Your stated aim might be something along the lines: 'To talk about our engagement to date and some potential opportunities for the future.'

By way of results, you might use ideas such as:

- so that I can understand how you feel this is going so far and any changes of direction you might have in mind;
- I can outline some longer term opportunities for you that I can see, based on our work together; and
- we can agree whether and if so how I might be able to help you to achieve those results.

You may well have asked questions about how the client defines their success during your initial meeting; indeed that might have been part of the genesis of this engagement. Rather than repeat the question, you might repeat back the answers that the client gave you and ask if they still hold good or may have changed as a result of the engagement to date.

Based on what the client tells you, you can then either build on what has been said or offer your own vision of what might be possible and why. You may decide only to articulate in any detail an interim aim rather than the final end game as you see it. That would be appropriate if the client is experiencing some form of confidence issue or is blocked in their current role. At this point the client may well need further explanation and time to reflect.

Before the end of the coaching engagement you will need to have an explicit conversation – again probably outside the confines of a coaching session – about how the client wants to proceed. Assuming that they wish to work with you to achieve the aims that you have discussed, you can then talk about the mechanics such as fee arrangements plus the expected duration and process of engagement.

In terms of duration, I recommend that you contract for a 12-month period in the first instance and set an expectation that the engagement will probably last longer (if that is the case). However, it will be harder for most clients to make a commitment beyond 12 months as that (for many businesses) now represents a medium-term planning horizon. I will often contract for 12 months but invoice fees quarterly with a break clause in the contract after six months. If you have misjudged the situation, that break clause can be useful from your point of view as much as from the client's. The fact that it exists will usually make it easier for the client to say 'yes' as it reduces the perceived risk of a further engagement.

If the client is employed in an organization it will almost certainly be necessary to gain the agreement of others unless the client is quite senior and either has control of a development budget that can cover their own needs or is willing to pay you out of their own pocket. The former situation is somewhat more complex. The client will usually need to sell the idea of further development internally although may need to avoid mention of the end-game in case it scares senior colleagues. You yourself will almost certainly need to support that internal sale with what amounts to a re-pitch of your services and a repositioning of your role. That of course raises your profile within the client firm and may lead to further work. On the other hand it will usually lead to further scrutiny by people in roles such as head of HR or senior line managers: be prepared!

In terms of fee arrangements, you will probably want to move to a retainer fee basis, where you are paid a set amount each month. You should expect the time spent with the client to vary significantly from month to month and it is likely that you will be underpaid (in terms of an hourly rate) for the first few months of the new engagement. However, that will almost certainly rectify itself over the full cycle. In the event that it does not, then within reason put it down to experience. The longer term benefits in terms of new business and referrals should outweigh any such issues.

Make a plan...

In a SCL approach, it is likely that your coaching will be more directive than it might usually be. You are after all 'leading' the client into areas that are probably outside their comfort zone and perhaps outside their experience to date; hence the earlier comment about the possibility of moving into a mentoring role rather than pure coaching. This changes the nature of the interaction with the client. You will need to provide any tools that they lack or otherwise enable them to obtain those tools, whether by guided reading, specific training courses etc.

It may be necessary to bring in others from your professional network to support your work with the client if they have expertise that you lack. For example, a key factor in the success of the client might be to understand online marketing including how to build a suitable website. If you (in all honesty) lack deep expertise in that area, it will be necessary to find someone that has it and can teach it rapidly and in a manner that is accessible to the client.

The mere fact that someone is an expert does not mean that they can teach others. You should therefore have personal experience of the teaching capacity of the expert and be certain that they can do the necessary job in a manner that is congruent with your own approach (although not necessarily identical). You will of course be vouching for the ability of the trainer when you bring them into your engagement so it is obviously important to select carefully, as if you were recruiting an associate rather than simply a supplier of services.

In order to maximize the success of your SCL approach, you will need to plan each step. My approach is to start from the agreed end game, identify the intermediate hurdles or milestones and then plan backwards from the end to ensure that each step accomplishes what is necessary to enable the successful completion of the next. This is a basic approach to project management although you will not normally need to get into project management technicalities or use specialist software such as MS Project: this is essentially common sense. Once you have built an outline plan with approximate time-frames and a list of steps required, number each workstream and each step within it. For example if one stream of work is about increasing the number of customers, this might be Workstream no 1. Steps within Workstream no 1 might include:

1.1 Develop a referral programme for the website

1.2 Online PPC advertising programme

1.3 Offline advertising in trade press

Each sub-step would then be numbered 1.1.1, 1.2.1 etc. The benefit of numbering each step is that it makes it easier to discuss issues over the phone. The numbers act as a form of shorthand and avoid a breach of confidentiality if the conversation happens to be overheard. Obviously both parties must be looking at the same document for this to work effectively. You will no doubt wish to share your project plan or summary sheet with the client. Indeed, in my view it is best to build the plan with them (to 'co-develop' it) so that it is as much 'their' plan as yours; indeed they should rapidly come to treat it as their own. At each step, you will need to identify not only what the client needs to achieve but what you must deliver in order to ensure success. I recommend a structured (but short) review at the end of each stage before you move on to the next. This should be an opportunity for celebration as well as ticking off tasks that have been completed. In my experience celebration of success tends to reinforce it and to enhance the pace of development.

Running the plan

Once you adopt a SCL approach with a given client the nature of the engagement changes. Rather than responding to the client's statements on goals and blocking factors as you might in a typical, non-directive coaching session, for example, you will need to reframe the goals etc (where necessary) in the context of the plan you and the client have made to get to the agreed end state. Your leadership is therefore:

- enabling the client to understand that they have potential they had not previously recognized;
- enabling the client to give themselves permission to succeed at that level;
- co-developing a workable plan to achieve an agreed end state; and
- keeping the delivery against that plan on track but dynamic (ie it can change as circumstances demand).

Not all coaches wish to adopt this type of approach as it differs too much from the comfort zone of their training and experience.

Clearly all of this is more demanding than a typical coaching engagement both in terms of time commitment for both you and the client and also in terms of the toolkit you deploy. Your fee rates will need to reflect this, including the opportunity cost to you of not having the time to take on additional 'normal' (ie non-SCL) clients. You will also need to factor in a need for continual review of your work with any SCL client in order to ensure that the approach is still valid and that both you and the client are gaining the appropriate level of value. It can be tempting to keep a SCL relationship going beyond its natural end. To do so can erode the perceived value to the client and can make you complacent about future fee income. For the latter reason alone it is worth ending this type of engagement promptly. Not only is it more likely that the client will come back for more when the time is right but you also avoid becoming stale in the working relationship and force yourself to seek new business continually. That is vital if your own business is not to stagnate.

Finally...

You do not need to seek out clients with whom you can follow a SCL approach in order to have a successful coaching business. As outlined above, there is a cost in terms of time and effort in moving to SCL with a given client and you need to be happy with the cost/benefit outcomes for your own business before you go forward. However, if you relish the idea of stretching yourself in your coaching and bringing into play other aspects of your knowledge and experience, this can represent an opportunity to do just that. It also changes your role with the relevant clients and can act as a lever to increase fee rates in other parts of your business, or to create a tiered offering where certain clients follow a different engagement pattern: a 'premium versus standard' model if you like. I offer the idea of SCL as an extension to your core business, recognizing that it can become a business model in its own right and locks out competitors.

And so to our final chapter, which covers the creation of a systems-led approach to your business.

CHAPTER SUMMARY

- Strategic client leadership (SCL) differs from the more commonly used strategic account management (SAM) in that it focuses on the individual client rather than the organization in which they work.

- Few clients will qualify for SCL and it is usually a mistake to encourage individuals towards this type of relationship unless you are truly convinced that (a) you want to do so; and (b) the client is truly capable of benefiting. Otherwise you risk setting inappropriate levels of expectation and consequent disappointment if these cannot be met.

- The use of the relationship pyramid helps to define both where you are in terms of your client relationship and also the potential for the relationship. It is effective only to the extent that your assessments are realistic.

- In starting the process of leading the client towards a more strategic approach in your work with them, tread carefully at first. There is the obvious risk of confusion of role and of causing confusion. It is usually best of that initial conversation is held informally with your vision of the client's potential exposed only in part.

- In taking forward an SCL approach, it will usually be necessary to move to a retainer fee approach rather than a 'per session' or 'per hour' fee arrangement. Not least, that sets up a different role for you with that client.

- Once you have agreement from the client to proceed towards SCL, make a project plan and monitor progress against that plan. Share this with the client when appropriate.

- Don't force the fit: SCL is not for everyone.

Systems set your business free

11

This final chapter is aimed at those who want to minimize friction in their business; who seek to build a 'real' business that can be expanded and which can employ others (physically or virtually) if you wish. Even if you prefer to operate as a solo-preneur, a 'systematic' business delivers a platform that you can work 'on' rather than work 'in' and is a business in which success is planned rather than being achieved by chance. You avoid 'just winging it' and hence avoid stress, errors and a greater likelihood of failure. If you build your business as a set of linked systems, you create something that is designed to operate correctly (ie to produce the results you expect) most of the time. When the unexpected occurs, you can rapidly identify what went wrong and fix it. However, you fix it not just for this occasion but also for the future because you adjust the system (ie fix the root cause) rather than just fixing the symptoms you see.

The term 'systems' here is not simply about the use of technology (although some use of technology will probably be helpful). It is about the development of a systemic mind-set for the operation of your business that helps you to eliminate guesswork as much as possible, avoids the need to remember 'stuff' (and hence minimizes distractions) and allows you to focus on the core activities of finding good potential clients, connecting with them positively, winning business and delivering excellent coaching. As a result, you save considerable time and wasted effort.

In this chapter, the focus is not on outsourcing (although outsourcing, like effective IT systems, may be helpful), but on putting in place the systems and processes that would enable successful outsourcing if and when you decide to do it. Those same systems and processes can also allow you to bring associates and others into your business more easily if you wish and ensure that they are able to achieve whatever tasks they need to accomplish to a standard that is similar to your own.

Why systems?

Essentially, systems in your business avoid the need for guesswork and, more importantly, the need to remember to carry out routine tasks, which can act as a drag to doing those tasks that are actually important in taking your business forward. The result is to minimize errors and the sort of 'loose ends' that tend to act as a drag on most businesses and indeed the personal lives of most people. You will tend to get more done, make more money and experience less stress if your business is built around systems. The systems in your business come about through the thinking that enables you to create three sets of documents:

- your statement of strategic aims;
- your business operating principles; and
- the standard operating procedures (SOPs).

Design from the end backwards

Before you start to design and build the systems that will support your business, it is important to do a little forward thinking in order that you can then backwards plan. That may sound counterintuitive. However, you will need to be able to develop your systems so far as possible in the context of what the business is to become in the medium term (say one to two years or so) rather than where it is today. In most cases the systems you create in that context will continue to be viable indefinitely, although there may be changes of scale.

For example, if your computer backup system involves the use of a USB connected external hard drive today, that may be replaced in due course by a NAS drive or even a small server with two or more drives in RAID configuration. The change of hardware will be driven by the scale of your business – its complexity increases as the business becomes larger. That in turn will change the detail of the procedure that you put in place but not the need for a backup process and one that, ideally, does not rely on you remembering to do it manually.

A starting point would be to project what you wish the business to look like when it becomes truly successful. You can then begin to work out what sort of infrastructure would be needed and hence the sort of processes and systems that would need to be in place. Design the business and the processes and procedures that support it as if you were creating a franchise where you would need to list all the functions, roles and responsibilities and then describe how each is to be performed. Even if yours is (and will remain for the foreseeable future) a one person business, where the person accountable and responsible for all tasks is you, it is important to identify what needs to be done routinely in order that the business can function effectively. If you build processes and procedures to ensure that the routine 'stuff' is handled as a routine, you can then focus on the exceptions. The result is to minimize routine items becoming problems that require real attention.

This is akin to driving a car. When you learn to drive you are aware of every change of gear, application of the brakes and turn of the steering wheel. It feels hard to drive even a short distance. When the vast majority of the driving process becomes routine and requires no conscious thought, it is easier to drive further and more quickly without felt stress. It is also easier to spot exceptions/problems and react quickly to take avoiding action, because the process of driving does not act as a distraction from spotting problems.

In thinking about the systems that underlie your business, it will help to adopt a common platform wherever possible; rather like using a spreadsheet program and a word processor that are compatible. Consistency of approach is also important.

The statement of strategic aims: what is my business?

It is hard to begin to build systems unless you are clear in your own mind about your strategic aim for the business. This should be written down before you start on anything else and should not, ideally, need to change to any extent – if at all – over time although you should review it periodically.

It is not simply a 'mission statement'; indeed many corporate mission statements tend to obfuscate rather than clarify. (The website of Scott Adams, the creator of the cartoon character Dilbert, used to have an automatic 'Mission Statement Generator' which, on clicking a button, produced random collections of business school gobbledegook that looked scarily real as examples of corporate mission statements.)

In this case the strategic aim defines the purpose of your business in simple terms. It should not be longer than two typewritten pages and ideally a single page. It should cover in bullet point form what your business is, the values it espouses and how it will feel to be a client (or staff member). It should also cover the kind of values and behaviours that define good clients and good staff members. The latter represents a line in the sand for you yourself even if you do not currently plan to employ others.

As an outline, your strategic aims document could cover the following points:

- 'Who we are';
- your basic business strategy;
- the principles that guide your business;
- what the business does;

- the main factors that drive the success of the business;

- the competitive advantages of the business (ie answers to the second killer question: 'What makes you different?');

- any specific commitments that define your approach to doing business (for example willingness to challenge yourself and clients etc);

- a statement about who are your preferred clients (ie essentially part of the answer to the first killer question 'What do you do?' which we explored in Chapter 2).

You might want to include points such as functions you will out-source: for example book-keeping and financial control if you plan to do that in the foreseeable future. A subsidiary benefit of writing this document is that some or all of it can become part of your website copy and part of your marketing collateral.

Who we are

This can be a single sentence that defines how you wish to be perceived by clients. In the previous chapter, this was expressed as a statement to the effect 'We seek to be recognized as...' that identifies the role you seek. Whether you use the phrase 'We seek to be...' or the more vigorous version 'We are...' is a matter of personal choice. If you can say with confidence: 'We are...', so much the better. However, when starting a business you may feel it more authentic to use the 'We seek to be...' form.

Your basic business strategy

This is a simple, high-level statement of how you will go about your business. It might be as simple as: 'The strategy of this business is to be rigorous in using my knowledge and experience of coaching for the benefit of my clients in the XYZ field, plus the systems I have designed in order to build the business most effectively.' An even simpler alternative might be: 'The strategy of the business is to use my coaching expertise and the systems I have devised rigorously in order to deliver maximum benefit for my carefully selected clients.'

The principles that guide the business

This is not a bland 'motherhood and apple pie' set of statements, nor is it the same as your business operating principles, which we look at below. This is a concrete set of commitments that cover your values and behaviours plus the way in which you go about your business etc. Try not to clutter the strategic aims document with more tactical items. The guiding principles in this strategic aims document can cover items such as:

- a commitment to flexibility of approach but not to negotiable values;

- a commitment to building and following a systematic approach that can be adjusted to cater for changing circumstances; and

- a commitment to use the procedures that underpin the systems of the business (without procedures there is no system...).

What the business does

This might seem to be a blinding glimpse of the obvious. Surely it's just another coaching business? In this case it really is not quite that simple. This is a reminder of what you do for clients, expressed in terms of the benefits/results you seek to deliver. It sets the parameters of your business and reminds you where the boundaries of your business activity lie. A benefit of this statement is to prevent distractions in building your business; knowing what opportunities you will not follow.

As an example of a failure to follow this basic boundary setting, a friend of mine ran a successful international coaching and consulting business for many years. He had considerable previous military experience and found an opportunity to set up a security business combining (among other things) physical security of premises, close protection of individuals and the training of individuals in the avoidance of conflict situations, possible kidnapping etc. Having spent more than two years in developing this idea in parallel with his core business, it produced very limited results. His original core business had lost traction, because he had been unable to devote the same degree of focus to both opportunities at the same time.

I suggest phrasing this statement along the lines: 'The principle business of [XYZ] is...' In my own business: 'The principle business of DLO Development is to enable coaches, business owners and fee-earners in professional firms to enhance their marketing and business development capabilities and hence profitability.'

Factors that drive the success of the business

This section is not quite the same as statements about competitive advantage. It can best begin with the phrase 'Our success depends on...'. It sets out the things that must be present in order that the business can succeed. For example:

Our success depends on:

1 an effective approach to identifying and connecting with the right kind of clients including effective generation of referrals to our preferred types of client;

2 a robust methodology to qualify those potential clients so that we minimize wasted effort;

3 ascertaining rapidly and with a high degree of accuracy what drives each client emotionally so that a tailored, value driven proposal can be made which resonates with the client and maximizes the probability they will say 'yes';

4 delivering excellent value to each client linked explicitly to the needs and success measures they identified in our initial meeting and developed subsequently;

5 an effective customer relationship management (CRM) system that enables appropriate levels of relevant contact to be maintained with each client long term.

Each of these points will need a system to be put in place to ensure that it can be achieved easily and repeatably.

Competitive advantages

This section answers the question 'What makes you different?'. That might include some of your 'values and behaviours' statements, plus some statements about the mechanics of the way in which you operate. For example: 'We challenge clients to achieve more than they thought possible and hold them to account vigorously for achieving the aims that they have set themselves.' It might also refer to any proprietary tools or protocols that you have developed. If you work with a specific type of client (for example senior women in professional firms) and you yourself have direct experience in that kind of role, you might usefully cover here how you will leverage that experience.

Specific commitments

In this section you can cover any items that you undertake to deliver in order to build and sustain your business. For example:

- in order to build our business, we will take on only those clients where there is a sound personal fit and also an excellent commercial fit – ie where we can make a significant positive impact on their success;

- we undertake to build systems into our business that minimize errors and maximize the value we deliver for clients;

- we will undertake continuing professional and personal development, including regular supervision, in order to keep knowledge current and hence deliver maximum value for clients.

Who are your preferred clients?

This is an output from the work we explored in Chapter 2 on defining a 'perfect' client for you. This is something that may develop over time but should not change radically unless the nature of the whole business is to change also. If that becomes the case, it may be sensible to consider setting up a separate, parallel business that focuses on the new client type. Each type of client will have specific needs depending on their field of work or the nature of the issues they seek to address. Your approach may need to vary similarly.

Business functions

In this last section of your strategic aims document, you may want to add a section on the functions to be carried out within the business and those that are to be (or could be) outsourced. It may be that you do everything in the business today. However, by identifying the relevant functions needed to operate the business you enable yourself more easily to identify what is to be outsourced in future. This also gives you an outline to begin building the next set of systems documents, which are the operating principles for the business.

It is of course possible to group some of the above sections together in order to shorten the document. You may decide to omit some of them or to cover the relevant ideas in the business operating principles, which we explore below.

Business operating principles

This second document is a more tactical description of the way in which your business works; essentially 'How we work here'. In combination with the strategic aims document, it would give someone like a new person joining your business a clear idea of what it feels like to work with you. It will also outline how decisions are taken and what takes priority. These ideas are as valuable to you in informing the decisions you take as the owner of the business as they would be for employees if and when you have them. This document could also provide general guidance on how to resolve problems that might occur.

As examples, your business operating principles could cover things such as:

- Avoiding grey areas of responsibility, which tend to allow problems to develop. This will be achieved by developing and adhering to robust SOPs.

- Avoiding a need to fight fires in the business by identifying and addressing the root causes of potential problems.

- Using problems as learning opportunities to prevent recurrence. This is done by adjusting existing procedures or developing new ones.

- Engaging in planned personal and professional development for xx per cent of your working time each month, by way of formal courses, supervision and/or reading. (This could/should be extended to all staff in the business as and when you employ others.)

- A focus on simplicity so far as possible and limiting the scope of the business to what is realistic, manageable and achievable.

- A commitment to seriousness of purpose but levity of approach.

- Developing and using documented procedures that can be followed by non-experts and incorporating these into your SOPs.

- Avoiding procrastination (for example by handling any incoming document or e-mail on the same day by way of the '4D' approach (Do it, Defer it (with a specific date), Delegate it (with a specific date) or Drop it) and also completing each and every task rather than leaving it part done).

- Maintaining effective and relevant contact with clients and potential clients, using automation and technology to minimize direct input on your part.

- Focus on tasks that are important versus those that are urgent (in the eyes of others). (This can be achieved through effective time allocation and task prioritization.)

These ideas are simple in themselves but if followed through they are powerful guidelines for the running of your business. Once you have the strategic aims and the operating principles clear in your mind and written down, you can begin to think through the SOPs.

Standard operating procedures (SOPs)

SOPs are the day-to-day guidelines that will ensure that your business 'just works' routinely. This concept is borrowed from the military. SOPs represent 'how we do what we do around here' and give guidance on how to carry out tasks and handle problems. They also serve to minimize the occurrence of problems. In the military context, SOPs represent a combination of recognized good practice and a set of instructions. The benefit is that nobody has to think about how to proceed when there is an emergency. When troops go into action, especially in a situation where civilians are also present (for example on the streets of Northern Ireland in the 1970s and '80s during the Troubles) there is a SOP to be followed when they come under fire. So long as that SOP is followed, a soldier who fires back at the attacker can expect to be acting in accordance with the law and civilian casualties will be avoided so far as possible.

Each procedure needs to be:

- simple to understand and to follow;
- linear (ie in step by step format); and
- complete (including any links to previous or following steps, especially if, for example, you cannot start Step B until Step A has been completed and, once complete, Step B leads to Step C).

The test for any new SOP is whether someone unfamiliar with the process can follow what has been written and carry out the process successfully. I typically ask a family member to read through each SOP to ensure that it passes that test. Your SOPs should also be open to amendment. That does not mean they can be imprecise or that they are optional; simply that, if you find a better way of doing something, you should be willing to change the procedure accordingly.

In a one-person business, it may seem like overkill to develop and document SOPs. However, rather in the same way as it is said that the best way to understand a topic is to teach it to others, the process of writing a set of SOPs is a great way to make sure that each process is well thought through and robust. It avoids having to reinvent the wheel each time a given situation arises and saves the need to remember things. It puts you in the position of the experienced driver who can undertake a car journey without thinking about each step. Try to limit each SOP to a single page. This is easier if you break down each process to a reasonably granular level without reducing it to minutiae.

Writing your SOPs

I recommend that you think about the business as a series of 'topics'; for example:

- marketing and sales;
- building your professional network;
- fee arrangements and billing;
- creating proposals;
- preparation and follow-up for sessions;
- client relationship management;
- computer data backup; and
- record keeping and financial control;

Within each topic area, consider the results that you want to achieve and then the steps or processes that need to be carried out in order to achieve those results. You now have a list of SOPs for that topic area. Where practicable, put these into chronological sequence. You can then begin to write each SOP in turn. Keep the SOP to a level of detail that is helpful to you and would enable a person of reasonable common sense to carry it out without help. The more detailed/granular the description, the more likely it is that either you will miss a minor step or that your description can be misinterpreted.

SOP template

In writing your SOPs, I suggest that you develop a standard template and use it for each SOP. Save the template and each of the SOPs to a specific folder on your computer. I find it helpful to use a sub-folder for each topic area. Use the header or footer to add a version number and date. I also add a copyright statement in case I decide to pass on any of my SOPs to clients. If I did do so, I would re-save the document in .pdf format to minimize the likelihood that it will be changed.

As an example, let us look at a simple SOP for backing up the data on your computer (see Table 11.1).

TABLE 11.1   Computer backup procedure

Aim	To ensure that all data and program files are backed up so that nothing is lost in the event of a computer failure.
Success factors	Data files are backed up daily.
	Data and program files are held in at least two separate locations, one of which is not in the same building as the computer being backed up
	Data and program files can be recovered in case of need within 24 hours with no loss of data.
	In the event of a computer failure, it is still possible to respond to client e-mails the same day.
Equipment required	2 × external USB-connected hard drives, each with the same (or larger) capacity as the hard drive of the computer to be backed up and with its own USB cable.
	Copy of Acronis True Image software on CD/DVD or Flash drive.
	Recovery disk or USB Flash drive with Windows operating system.
	Carbonite cloud storage account.
	E-mail-capable smartphone (to allow e-mail responses in the event that the computer fails, until repairs can be carried out and data restored).

TABLE 11.1   *continued*

Procedure for backup	Ensure that Acronis True Image software is loaded on the computer.
	Connect external USB hard drive.
	When the 'Options' table appears, click 'Open folders to view files' then minimize to the task bar.
	Open Acronis True Image Home by clicking the icon on the desktop.
	Select Backup, then My Disks.
	When prompted, select the external hard drive as the backup location.
	On the first backup each month, first wipe the external USB hard drive and then create a new backup. Otherwise add to the existing archive.
	Click Proceed. Once the backup is complete, disconnect the external USB hard drive and store it securely. One external drive is to be kept at the office, locked in a drawer or filing cabinet. The second backup drive is to be kept at home also locked in a drawer.
	This procedure is to be carried out at least weekly, on each of the two external hard drives; one on Tuesdays the other on Fridays.
	For online backup, go to **www.carbonite.com** and set up an account that provides sufficient space to hold all data files on the computer (program files are optional). Carbonite will back up any new or changed files whenever the computer is connected to the internet, hence providing daily backup.

You can of course create a similar SOP for the recovery process.

Note that there is a clear aim and a clear statement of success factors. The latter sets the standard to be achieved (in this case bi-weekly backup of data and program files plus daily backup of data files on-line). This helps you to decide how to go about the backup process. In this case there are two types of backup: the USB hard drives and the automated online backup. Two USB hard drives stored in different locations gives you 'belt and braces' and increases the likelihood of being able to lay your hands on one of the drives rapidly in case of need (I have one drive at my home office and the other at the office in London some 50 miles away). It also obviates the possibility of both drives being stolen or destroyed by fire at the same time.

Why not use Carbonite for all my backup needs? Because the speed of recovery is limited to the download capacity of my internet connection; so to recover a full set of data could take a couple of days. Also it is not clear to me that Carbonite will preserve the folder structure of the original hard drive. Lastly, the creation of a mirror image of my computer hard disk appears to obviate the need to reinstall program files with what might be attendant licensing issues. On the occasions I have had to go through the recovery process, the newly installed hard drive on my computer becomes a clone of the old one and the process is pretty much seamless. Is it necessary to explain all of this in the SOP? No, I don't believe so.

However, if you choose to add a covering note or a set of 'design factors' so be it.

Outsourcing

As a former colleague of mine said (many times!), 'You can't outsource crap'. In other words if a process is broken, not working smoothly or not well thought through, it cannot be outsourced successfully. The development of your SOPs allows you to outsource any element of your business because the person taking it over will have a clear statement of what is required (supported by your operating principles and strategic aims). By the same token, it is possible that the person to whom you outsource will have their own procedures that will produce the results you need and may indeed understand better than you do what those results are.

For example, I outsource all of my financial control, tax returns etc to my accountant. The SOP for that is simple: essentially putting together a package of hard copy receipts and incoming invoices etc each quarter by the end of the first working week. In order to give my accountant my business income data, I copy her on each invoice sent to a client. By the end of the first month in the quarter, she compiles the data, prepares the VAT return, runs a balance sheet for the business etc. I receive the figures by e-mail and sign off on them. She submits the relevant returns online and any tax due is then paid by direct debit.

All I need to document by way of the SOP is my part in this process: compiling the data and signing off on the figures. I would not presume to tell my accountant how to process the data and produce the returns; she knows far more about that than I do and I trust her implicitly to get the figures right. I do, however, keep watch on the bank balance and validate any payments myself. I also carry out a common sense 'gross error' check that the figures I see are in line with what I would reasonably expect.

When you outsource a function, the relevant SOP acts as a good starting point to define the relationship and the standards you expect to be achieved. Once you agree the outsourcing and how results are to be monitored, change your own SOP to reflect the monitoring process that you will now undertake and drop the previous 'how to do it' SOP. That does not mean that you delete it from your system completely; simply that it can go into a 'no longer current' folder. It may be necessary to resurrect it at some point in the future.

When you decide to outsource a function, it is important to record exactly what is to be outsourced and the results/standards to be expected on both sides. In many businesses this would be called a service level agreement or SLA. Once this is finalized, it should not be necessary to refer to the document again. If you do, there is a strong possibility that the relationship has broken down in some way. If that occurs more than once it may well be broken terminally.

Having documented all of the SOPs that you need for the business, you can then decide which functions you wish to outsource. As a rule of thumb, 'do only what only you can do' of course. However, in the early stages of running a business it may be that you do not have the cash flow to enable you to outsource very much. I suggest that you prioritize the functions that you wish to outsource and make a plan for each. Even if cash flow is tight, it may benefit you to outsource things that would occupy too much of your time or which you simply lack the knowledge to do successfully.

'Virtual' employees

Many small businesses now use 'virtual' staff; often in the form of a 'virtual assistant' (VA) who will take care of routine administration jobs, secretarial functions etc. That person may also be able to provide your telephone answering service and book train tickets or flights etc if required. I have limited experience in using a VA. However, if you are fortunate enough to find someone in that role who does an excellent job, look after them because, anecdotally, they may be the exception rather than the rule.

When you hire a VA (or any kind of virtual employee), I suggest that you start with a trial period of one or two months. During that time, take the opportunity to 'become your own customer' by making calls to your 'office' number (if telephone answering is part of the service), sending e-mail requests for information etc and assess the response you receive as if you were a key client. If it is less good than you expect, create or upgrade the relevant SOP and make adherence to your SOP a condition of continuing with the service. If the problems persist you will have to look elsewhere.

If possible arrange to meet the individual face to face and follow the 'like and trust' test as if you were a client. Take a look at the website of the VA (especially if the VA is an individual rather than a firm specializing in this service, as many are). Some years ago, I was approached by a VA both to hire her and to recommend her to others. I looked at her website to find that a significant part of it was devoted to her love of tattoos and the deep meaning they held for her. It included photos. This lady may have been technically excellent as a VA but the perceptions one gained from the website were not necessarily what she might have wished and certainly not how I wanted my own business to be seen. If the prospective VA is likely to have contact with your clients, even by phone, it is important that they portray your business as you wish it to be seen.

If the VA you hire is located in a different country, think about the issues of time difference and language (even if only in terms of accent if they are to answer your business phone number). I was surprised, for example, routinely to receive e-mails from the assistant of a client with time stamps in the early hours of the morning. It transpired that she was based in Australia; not a problem as such, just a surprise as I had gained the impression that the client's staff were based in London.

Core systems

You may decide that it is simply too onerous to develop systems to cover all aspects of your business, at least in the early stages. That is clearly something for you to decide. However, if you do nothing else, I highly recommend that you do spend the time to build systems covering three aspects:

- building your professional network (including winning clients);
- invoicing and financial control; and
- data backup.

If you focus on those elements of your business you will not go too far wrong. For my own business, I would add one more item, which is developing your marketing collateral.

Time allocation

The idea of time allocation has been mentioned several times in this book. This is based on a couple of key ideas:

- time cannot be managed, only allocated; and

- if a task is not in the diary, with reasonable time set aside, it is unlikely to be done.

If you are able to prioritize tasks and allocate the necessary time to them in a systematic manner, you obviate the incessant 'to do' list, where tasks migrate from one list to the next. You also give yourself permission to drop, delegate or defer tasks that are not in fact important but which may be considered urgent.

A basic approach to time allocation starts with capturing all the tasks you have on any of your 'to do' lists, plus any known routine or recurring items such as filling in and submitting financial returns, etc. You may wish to make an initial cut between different types of task. For example, if you have allocated two days each week to marketing and sales, it will help to bring together all the tasks related to those activities. If you have decided to spend one day per week on business administration and personal development, group together all the tasks that relate to those areas, etc.

The next step is to prioritize the task list for each area. I use three levels:

A = the task is a 'must do' item and typically has a deadline that is reasonably close: two to four weeks away.

B = the task is a 'should do' item and either has no deadline or the deadline is say three weeks or more away.

C = a 'would like to do' item with no immediate deadline (for example sorting and Photoshopping my digital photograph collection).

Tasks may move up or down the levels. For example, my tax return is a 'B' item for much of the year, but becomes an 'A' item at the beginning of January if my accountant has not already completed it.

Once tasks have been prioritized, you can decide how much time each of the A and B tasks will require to achieve a sound 'fit for purpose' result (as opposed to perfection). At this stage you can now allocate the necessary time.

You will need to set the start and end times for your working day, or at least the number of working hours you are willing to allocate. It is essential to allocate time for exercise, eating etc. You must also allow time for adequate sleep each day (sleep deprivation is used as an interrogation technique for a reason).

Break the working day into 15-minute slots. Allow yourself one slot at the start or the end of the day (I prefer the latter) to have a 'meeting with me', which is used to plan the day ahead or the day following. Allow a further one or two slots in the morning and the same in the afternoon to handle e-mails and phone calls. Slot in meetings as necessary (which should form part of your 'A' task list: if they are not A items it begs the question why you have agreed to attend). For the remaining time, at least 70 per cent should be allocated to A tasks. It may need to be 100 per cent. If there is time available, you can allocate up to 20 per cent to B items. If there is still time available then up to 10 per cent can be given to C items. The reality is that few if any C items will get done. That gives you permission to drop those items entirely or to delegate them.

A huge benefit of this mechanistic approach is that it forces you to be sparing with your time and to be realistic about what you undertake to deliver. It can hence save you from over-commitment.

In conclusion

The approach outlined in this book may seem to involve a huge amount of planning and preparation. The time needed to do this effectively, once the overall approach is understood and becomes part of your 'business as usual' process, is in fact quite small. The benefit is that you spend minimal time in wasted meetings and each conversation is purposeful. Clients rapidly come to recognize this and it tends to enhance your role in their eyes. They come to understand that you respect their time as much as you respect your own and that, if you ask for a three-minute phone call, you really mean three minutes. The other key benefit is to minimize the impact of chance so that you save time and can get more done. You succeed by design and not by accident.

Key to your overall success is high levels of activity focused on the right things:

- finding and connecting with the right kind of clients;
- assessing in each case the degree of 'fit' both personally and commercially;
- identifying value that you can deliver and which is relevant, right now, to the client;
- enabling the client to see that value and the consequent benefits/results for them;
- asking for the business;
- writing an effective letter of confirmation/proposal; and hence
- winning the procurement battle (or if possible ensuring that it does not take place).

Delivery of coaching is a bonus that you get as a reward for all the other hard work. A by-product of the approach outlined in this book is that you can begin to enjoy the journey that leads to successful coaching opportunities. There are no rules, but you now have a tested framework to support and guide you.

Enjoy the journey.

CHAPTER SUMMARY

- Developing a systems mind-set helps you to build systems that enable you to work on rather than in your business and minimizes the need to remember to carry out routine tasks. In addition to helping to avoid errors, this removes a source of distraction from your key, value adding activities – eg identifying good potential clients and generating revenue as well as delivering excellent coaching.

- Design your systems from the end backwards. Consider how the business will look, feel and operate in one to two years' time assuming that it is successful. Work back from that end point and design the systems that will be needed at that time and that will enable you to get there most effectively.

- Your statement of strategic aims sets the framework within which the business will operate and the boundaries around it. This should be able to remain largely unchanged over time and should ideally be limited to a single typed page, two at most.

- Your business operating principles represent high-level guidance on specific tasks and priorities. They help to set a context for your standard operating procedures (SOPs) as well as the tone for your business.

- SOPs must be simple, linear and complete. If any given SOP becomes unduly complex (longer than one page) it should probably be broken down into two or more separate SOPs.

- The aim and the relevant success factors are the critical starting points for each SOP.

- Use your SOPs as the basis for outsourcing functions. These can become the basis for an SLA where that is necessary (experience indicates that it almost always is, even if only to set expectations).

- Time cannot be managed, only allocated. Use a suitable task prioritization and diary management system to ensure that you allocate time to issues that are both important to the success of your business and urgent (or have a deadline) rather than merely urgent.

- Enjoy the journey.

INDEX

NB page numbers in *italic* indicate figures or tables

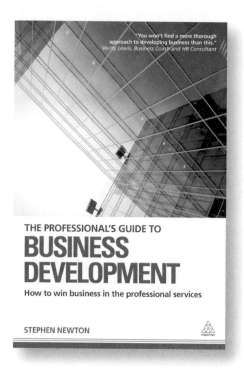